はじめに

　本書は、現代社会のキーワードである「ウェルビー◻◻◻◻◻◻◻◻◻◻◻◻した英語の総合教材です。ウェルビーイングは、一般的に「健康で幸福な暮らし」を意味し近年様々な文脈で見聞きすることが多くなっている言葉です。しかし、経済的に発展し社会基盤が整った日本で生活する私たちにとっては、幸せな生活を成り立たせる要因について踏み込んで考えてみる機会は少ないのではないでしょうか。価値観や生き方が多様化する現代の社会であるからこそ、幸せな暮らしという一見当たり前の概念に向き合うことが重要です。

　本書は、幸せな日々を過ごすために必要な要因について英語で学びながら、それらに関係する社会問題について、実際のニュース動画の視聴を通して知識を深め考えることができるようにデザインされています。昨今、ChatGPT をはじめとする生成 AI や機械翻訳の普及で教材の内容や使用法が見直されていますが、本書では使用するツールに左右されることなくアウトプット力を養い発展的な学習につなげていけるアクティビティが用意されています。学習者のみなさんには、英語力を伸ばすことはもちろん、日ごろ意識する機会が少ない自国以外の問題にも関心を持ち、主体的な学習へと発展させることができるようになってほしいものです。本書がその一助となれば幸いです。

▶▶ Warm Up Quizzes: Learning the Basics

単文の穴埋め問題を通して、各ユニットのトピックについての基礎知識を学びます。

🪷 Reading Activities

リーディングを通して、ウェルビーイングについての基礎知識や、Video Activities の動画で取り上げられている社会問題に関する理解を深めます。

🧘 Video Activities

動画クリップを視聴し、様々なスタイルの英語を通して現代社会が直面している課題について学び考えます。

💬 Exchanging Ideas and Thoughts

各ユニットのトピックに沿った会話演習で口頭のコミュニケーション力を伸ばし、会話の展開を考えることでアウトプット力を養います。

🔍 Further Activity

リーディングや動画で取り上げられているトピックや社会問題と関連の深い英語のウェブサイトを通してさらに知識を深め、主体的に発展的な学習に取り組む機会を提供します。

Well-being: Essential Elements for Our Life

CONTENTS

Copyrights in Video Activities

Unit 1: 'After five years we're getting used to it!' Finns react to 'world's happiest nation' status by ELIAS HUUHTANEN / AFPTV / AFP

Unit 2-3: With inflation at record highs, Sweden grapples with poverty by VIKEN KANTARCI / AFPTV / AFP

Unit 4: Africa feels economic fallout from Ukraine crisis by HICHAM RAFIH, AKIM REZGUI, GEORGE NTONYA, GLODY MURHABAZI, QUADRI TAIWO / AFPTV / UNTV / AFP

Unit 5: Uganda: food crises and hunger rife in Karamoja by TINA SMOLE / AFPTV / AFP

Unit 6: Myanmar's doctors on motorbikes trek dangerously to reach patients by RICHARD SARGENT / AFPTV / AFP

Unit 7: Ex racehorses provide comfort to children in need by CHARLOTTE TURNER / AFPTV / AFP

Unit 8: New mega-lab makes own weather to test homes of the future by WILLIAM EDWARDS / AFPTV / AFP

Unit 9 :Australia homelessness rising despite record beating economy by JUSTINE GERARDY, GLENDA KWEK / AFPTV / AFP

Unit 10: Ethiopia prepares for key vote amid war in Tigray, fears over fairness by SOLAN KOLLI, RAPHAEL AMBASU, EDUARDO SOTERAS / AFPTV / UNTV / WFP / AFP

Unit 11: Choking on factory waste: the Nile's rising scourge by TINA SMOLE / AFPTV / AFP

Unit 12: Threats and theft: The wretched life of C. Africa's peanut growers by CAROL VALADE, BARBARA DEBOUT / AFPTV / AFP

Unit 13: Learning to read and write at India's 'school for grannies' by PETER HUTCHISON / AFPTV / AFP

Unit 14: In London, a "death cafe" gives people safe space to discuss the finality of death by LINDA ABI ASSI / AFPTV / AFP

Unit 1 Measuring Well-being
健康で幸せな暮らしとは

▼ Introduction

心身ともに健康で幸せな暮らしのことをウェルビーイング (Well-being) と言います。このユニットでは、ウェルビーイングを測るための調査項目や、世界一幸せとされる国に住む人の声を踏まえて、幸福や満たされた人生について考えます。

▶▶ Warm Up Quizzes: Learning the Basics

Complete the sentences below and learn the basics about happiness and well-being.

(1) Well-being is the state of being physically, mentally, and emotionally healthy, content, and _____.

　　(A) fulfill　　　　(B) fulfilled　　　(C) fulfilling　　　(D) to fulfill

(2) It is not easy to identify _____ defines one's overall happiness.

　　(A) what　　　　(B) which　　　　(C) how　　　　(D) that

(3) People's values are changing as the world becomes increasingly _____.

　　(A) diversified　(B) diversifies　　(C) diversifying　(D) diversify

(4) Finland is known _____ being one of the happiest countries in the world.

　　(A) with　　　　(B) in　　　　　(C) to　　　　　(D) as

Reading Activities

Audio 1-02

Read the following passage.

1 Well-being is typically determined by factors such as health, happiness, and quality of life, and these factors can be evaluated according to specific indices. According to the report *How's Life* by the Organisation for Economic Co-operation and Development

5　(OECD), more than ten indices, including wealth and income, housing conditions, health status, education and skills, social connections, and others can be used to measure national well-being. The indices can be quantified, and meaningful comparisons of levels of well-being between different countries can be made.

10　**2** Other international organizations have also researched factors that determine well-being. The Sustainable Development Solutions Network, a global initiative by the United Nations (UN), produced The World Happiness Report on national and regional well-being. The report uses various factors, such as

15　economic indicators, social support systems, life expectancy, and freedom to make life choices, to measure well-being. Nordic countries such as Finland, Denmark, Norway, and Switzerland often have high rankings in the report. The report also identifies the overall happiest country in the world. Interestingly, Finland

20　has been recognized as the happiest country in the world on multiple occasions. This is because of its strong social welfare system, high standard of living, emphasis on education, and other factors.

3 The World Health Organization (WHO) has also developed a

25　self-report questionnaire that consists of five simple questions designed to assess an individual's emotional well-being and quality of life, called the WHO-5. **[1]**

　　1 "Over the last two weeks, how often have you felt cheerful and in good spirits?"

30　　2 "Over the last two weeks, how often have you felt calm and relaxed?"

　　3 "Over the last two weeks, how often have you felt active and vigorous?"

　　4 "Over the last two weeks, how often have you woken up

35　　feeling fresh and rested?"

　　5 "Over the last two weeks, how often have you felt interested in things?"

---

according to ~ ～によれば
indices indexの複数形
index 指標
organisation (organizationのイギリス英語綴り)
OECD 経済協力開発機構
wealth 財産、資産
income 収入
measure 測る
quantify 数値化する

initiative 取り組み

UN 国際連合、国連

economic indicator 経済指標
life expectancy 平均寿命
Nordic 北欧の

be recognized as ～と認められている
multiple occasions 複数回、何度も
welfare 福祉
emphasis on 重点を置くこと
WHO 世界保健機関
questionnaire アンケート
consist of ～から成る
assess 評価する、決める
in good spirits 上機嫌な元気な

vigorous 活発な、はつらつとした

rested 疲れていない、休息がとれた

4 [2] Each question was rated on a 6-point scale, ranging from 0 (never) to 5 (most of the time). [3] The WHO-5 is based on the concept that individual well-being can be captured by measuring positive emotions and overall life satisfaction. [4]

5 **5** Although there have been several attempts to define well-being, it is true that there is no absolute set of factors or list of questions that can fully evaluate it. It is therefore important to not only learn about recent developments about how to evaluate well-being, but also to think on a personal level about what 10 factors can make our own lives healthier and more fulfilling.

6-point scale	6段階評価
concept	考え、概念
attempt	試み
define	決める、定義する
absolute	絶対の
therefore	したがって
fulfilling	充実した

▶▶ Reading Comprehension 1

Read through the text and choose the correct answer.

1. What is the passage mainly about?
    a) How to set up valid questions to measure well-being
    b) Ways to measure well-being
    c) How to develop a research project to measure well-being
    d) Different definitions of well-being

2. Why are Nordic countries mentioned in the second paragraph?
    a) Because their social welfare systems are well-developed.
    b) Because they are considered to be happy countries.
    c) Because their economies are stable.
    d) Because housing conditions are outstanding.

3. What is the WHO-5?
    a) A group of five major international organizations working on issues related to well-being
    b) A checklist of serious international issues being addressed by the WHO
    c) An annual report by the WHO about well-being
    d) A set of questions to measure individual well-being

4. In which position from [1] to [4] does the following sentence best fit?
    "The five questions are as follows: "
    a) [1]   b) [2]   c) [3]   d) [4]

▶▶ Reading Comprehension 2

Answer the following questions in a complete sentence.

1. Describe the WHO-5 in a single sentence.
    (five questions / and level of life / to measure / a set of / it is / an individual's positive feelings / satisfaction).

2. Out of the five different indices introduced in the first paragraph, which one do you think is the most important for your well-being?

___

  **Video Activities**

🔊 Audio 1-03

▷ True or False Questions

Watch the video and check the facts. Circle T if the statement is true or F if it is false.

1. The video is mostly about the World Happiness Report. [T / F]
2. People in the video are not satisfied with the report. [T / F]
3. People in the video are from Switzerland. [T / F]
4. Beautiful nature contributes to the Finns' sense of well-being. [T / F]

▷ Comprehension Questions

Watch the video again and choose the correct answer. Read the script if necessary.

1. What is true about the World Happiness Report?
   a) It is partly based on how people assess their own happiness.
   b) The report's social data is collected from northern Europeans.
   c) The report's happiness-score scale is from zero to five.
   d) It first listed Finland as the happiest country in 2022.

2. Which of the following statements about the first interviewee is correct?
   a) He is planning to found a company because the economy recently improved.
   b) He had not heard of the happiness report before the interview.
   c) He understands why his country is ranked high in the report.
   d) He thinks the Russian invasion of Ukraine affected the outcome of the report.

3. What does the second interviewee say about her country?
   a) The climate has something to do with people's lifestyle.
   b) The small population of the country contributes to how happy people's lives are.
   c) Affordable housing is the key to being able to live happily.
   d) The social welfare system of her country is one of the best in the world.

Residents of Helsinki ¹( ) to the publication of the 2022 World Happiness Report, which named Finland as the world's happiest country for the fifth ²( ) year. The World Happiness Report is based on people's own assessment of their happiness, as well as economic and ³( )
5 data. Northern Europeans once again dominated the top spots with the Danes second behind the Finns, followed by the Icelandic, the Swiss and the Dutch.

The report raised some eyebrows when it first placed Finland at the top of its listings in 2018. But the country of ⁴( ) forests and lakes is also known for its well-functioning public services, ubiquitous saunas, widespread trust in
10 authority and low levels of crime and inequality.

Jukka Viitasaari: "I wasn't really surprised to find that Finns describe themselves as happy. Many things are undeniably good here—beautiful nature, we're well
15 governed, lots of things are in order."
"When we first won five years ago it was a big surprise, I must admit. We didn't notice day to day that things were in good shape, it was only when someone
20 from outside told us that we had it good compared to lots of other places. But after five years of coming top we're getting used to it!"

Hanna Liekso: "Maybe it's because in a cold
25 country you can't afford to waste energy on superficial things, so we focus on the important things. Lots of foreigners I know say that it takes time to get to know a Finn, but under the hard shell
30 you find a warm heart."

Jani: "During the winter also we can enjoy it, with the snow and skiing, doing sports outside. It ⁵( ) the people."

Exchanging Ideas and Thoughts

Practice the conversation with your partner. Think about how you can develop the conversation further.

A: I thought that happiness was just a feeling, but now I know that there are lots of factors that can make us feel happy or unhappy.

B: Yes, (1) 同じことを考えていました _____.
Do you think Japan would rank high on the World Happiness Report?

A: (2) かなり高いと思います _____. Housing is quite good, there is free education until university, and the healthcare system is of a high standard too.

B: True. On the other hand, people working at Japanese companies have to do a lot of overtime, and that might make people feel less happy.

A: Good point. I suppose having a good work-life balance would affect your level of happiness.

B: Yes. And it's something we need to keep in mind when we start our own careers.

 ## Further Activity

(1) Visit the following website to learn about the World Happiness Report and its ranking. Take notes and share some interesting facts and figures you find with your classmates.

World Happiness Report, Ranking of Happiness 2020-2022

 https://worldhappiness.report/ed/2023/world-happiness-trust-and-social-connections-in-times-of-crisis/#ranking-of-happiness-2020-2022

(2) Using key words and/or phrases you have learned from the reading and video, try Cinii Research or a similar information retrieval system to find some books and articles that are of interest to you. Compare your list of books and articles with your classmates' lists.

Unit 2 Financial Stability 1

お金とウェルビーイング

▼ Introduction

現代社会では、生活必需品の購入や快適な日常生活を送るために収入や蓄えが必要です。このユニットでは、毎日の生活の中で感じる幸せと人生全体で考えた時の幸福や、収入と幸福感の関係について知識を深め、お金がウェルビーイングに与える影響について考えます。

▶ Warm Up Quizzes: Learning the Basics

Complete the sentences below and learn the basics about financial stability in terms of well-being.

(1) Having money certainly _____ towards an individual's sense of well-being.

   (A) concludes   (B) confronts   (C) conducts   (D) contributes

(2) Money is essential for meeting basic needs such as food, shelter, healthcare, and education, and _____ a foundation for overall well-being.

   (A) provide   (B) provides   (C) providing   (D) provided

(3) Achieving a balance between financial stability and other important aspects of life is _____ to maximizing well-being.

   (A) chimney   (B) key   (C) attorney   (D) journey

(4) Money is not the sole _____ of happiness or overall life satisfaction.

   (A) determine   (B) determines   (C) determinant   (D) determination

🪷 Reading Activities

Read the following passage.

1 Financial stability is an important component of well-being. Being financially stable means having enough money to buy daily necessities, such as food, clothes, utility costs, household goods, and being able to pay housing expenses, such as rent or
5 a mortgage. **[1]** Money can buy many things that we need in life, but an important question we should ask ourselves is: does having a lot of money actually enhance our sense of well-being?

2 When we talk about well-being, we must distinguish between different aspects of well-being, such as emotional well-being and
10 life satisfaction. Emotional well-being, or experienced well-being, refers to the experiences of daily life that can be characterized as pleasant or unpleasant. Emotional well-being derives from various feelings or psychological reactions, such as joy, sadness, anger, affection, pride, boredom, and stress. **[2]** Life satisfaction,
15 or evaluative well-being, on the other hand, is about how we evaluate our life as a whole when we think about it.

3 According to a survey in 2010 of 1,000 US residents by Daniel Kahneman and Angus Deaton, happiness in terms of emotional quality increases in line with one's income until the annual
20 income reaches a threshold of $75,000. Pointedly, beyond the $75,000 per year threshold, incomes do not tend to enhance happiness any further.

4 On the other hand, a recent study by Matthew Killingsworth in 2021 suggested that happiness does not in fact hit a ceiling at an
25 income threshold of $75,000 per year. Drawing on approximately 1.7 million reports from more than 33,000 US adults, this study showed that higher incomes tend to lead to greater emotional well-being and life satisfaction even beyond the $75,000 threshold level.

5 While further research may be able to show in detail
30 how wealth and income affect emotional well-being and life satisfaction, there is already a clear and strong correlation between money and happiness. For instance, in terms of mental health, it has been observed that money can reduce stress from events that cause worry or anxiety. **[3]** Whilst it is true that
35 everyone faces a number of daily frustrations, when people have a higher income, they have more control over stressful events and therefore do not experience so much of a negative impact.

---

necessity 必要なもの
utility costs 光熱費
household goods 家庭用品、生活雑貨
expense 費用
enhance 高める
distinguish 区別する

pleasant 快適な
unpleasant 不快な
derive from ～に由来する
psychological reaction 心理的反応
affection 愛情
boredom 退屈、倦怠
survey 調査
resident 住人
annual income 年収
threshold 基準値、境界値

hit a ceiling 頭打ちになる
draw on ～を活用した

in detail 詳しく、詳細に

correlation 相互関係、相関
in terms of ～の観点では

worry 心配
anxiety 不安

This is because their access to financial resources provides them with more options for dealing with problems. **[4]** Although money does not buy everything, it is certainly a crucial factor in our overall well-being.

financial resources
金融資産、財力
options 選択肢
deal with 対処する、取り組む

 Reading Comprehension 1

Read through the text and choose the correct answer.

1. What is the passage mainly about?
   a) Goods and services that money can buy
   b) Advice on how to spend money wisely
   c) Mental disorders caused by financial insecurity
   d) Studies on the correlation between money and happiness

2. Which of the following exemplifies *emotional well-being*?
   a) A large bank balance
   b) Entertainment expenses used for business purposes
   c) The pleasant or unpleasant experiences of day-to-day life
   d) Disposable personal income

3. The word "hit" in paragraph 4, line 2, means
   a) to reach a particular number
   b) to experience troubles
   c) to attack something or someone
   d) to touch someone or something quickly and forcefully

4. In which position from **[1]** to **[4]** does the following sentence best fit?
   "It also means being able to pay for services such as public transportation, medical care, education, postal services, and the Internet also have a financial cost."
   a) **[1]**   b) **[2]**   c) **[3]**   d) **[4]**

 Reading Comprehension 2

Answer the following questions in a complete sentence.

1. What is emotional well-being based on?
   (in / on / our daily life / it is / based / various feelings)

_____

2. Name seven different feelings or emotions that affect emotional well-being in alphabetical order.

_____

 **Video Activities**

▶▷ True or False Questions

Watch the video and check the facts. Circle T if the statement is true or F if it is false.

1. The story is about public transport in Stockholm.   [T / F]
2. People are lining up for free breakfasts.   [T / F]
3. Kawian Ferdowsmi is in need of aid.   [T / F]
4. Today, Sweden is famous for its stable economy.   [T / F]

▶▷ Comprehension Questions

Watch the video again and choose the correct answer. Read the script if necessary.

1. What can you tell about people in need in Stockholm, Sweden?
   a) The number of homeless people has been decreasing.
   b) Most cases of homelessness in Stockholm have little to do with Sweden's economic conditions.
   c) The number of people in need has been increasing.
   d) There are not so many homeless people, but many people are facing financial problems.

2. What do you know about the economy in Sweden?
   a) It was weak in the past, but now it is very stable.
   b) It is one of the strongest in Europe.
   c) Activities by non-profit organizations play an important role in the economy.
   d) It is projected to get worse.

3. Which of the following is true?
   a) Usually, residents in major cities like Stockholm are the most affected by national economic conditions.
   b) Investing in public transit infrastructure is key to maintaining a strong economy.
   c) When a country is in recession, the government must provide citizens with adequate housing and food.
   d) In the beginning, energy prices and imports were most affected by inflation.

▶▷ Watch the video and complete the script.

It's just past six in the morning. And ¹( ) this train station in Stockholm, the city's homeless are already silently forming a long queue. Everyday, ²( ) people come here for breakfast: cinnamon pastries and a cup of coffee. Kavian Ferdowsi, who started this initiative, says the number of people ³( ) is now hitting record levels.

Kavian Ferdowsi: "As you see so many people coming here to the breakfast, during these thirteen years that I run this non-profit organization Homeless.Life. We never had so much people. That's why I can see that much more people now are coming to the line to us, much more people are coming here to get the food and to getting a simple help! We living in a very rich country but society became much poorer now and people need help!"

For a long time, Sweden has ⁴( ) one of the EU's most economically stable members. Now, according to the European commission, it's the only member state forecasted to go into recession this year, with inflation reaching records highs of ⁵( ) percent.

Annika Alexius: "So the first wave of inflation was just energy prices and some import prices. But now that has spread to the entire economy so we have the broad layers of prices increasing. You have, especially the lower income households put much more of their income into those two things: housing and food. And those two parts of the budget has increased, the prices have increased enormously."

Exchanging Ideas and Thoughts

Practice the conversation with your partner. Think about how you can develop the conversation further.

A: I hadn't ever really thought about the difference between experienced well-being and life satisfaction.

B: Me neither. And it's interesting that both are affected by financial stability, isn't it?

A: Yes, it is. (1) お金で幸せが買えると思いますか？ _____?

B: (2) 考えてみるのにいい質問ですね。 _____.
What do you think?

A: Well, we need money to fulfill our basic needs. So, we can't really say, "we don't need money to be happy."

B: You're right. Money isn't everything, but we have to be realistic about its importance for our well-being.

 **Further Activity**

(1) Visit the following website to learn about Income Distribution and Poverty in Japan from the world map. Focus on the Quality Reviews, take notes and share interesting facts and figures you find from the website with your classmates.

OECD Income (IDD) and Wealth (WDD) Distribution Databases

 https://www.oecd.org/social/income-distribution-database.htm

(2) Using key words and/or phrases you have learned from the reading and video, try Cinii Research or a similar information retrieval system to find some books and articles that are of interest to you. Compare your list of books and articles with your classmates' lists.

Unit 3 Financial Stability 2

景気と物価

▼ Introduction

個人の収入や資産は、社会の経済情勢に大きく影響を受けます。このユニットでは不景気やスタグフレーション等の基礎知識について学び、経済と個人の生活との関係について、スウェーデンの事例を踏まえて考えます。

▶▶ Warm Up Quizzes: Learning the Basics

Complete the sentences below and learn the basics about wealth and income in terms of well-being.

(1) Preserving people's wealth ensures that their living standards can be _____ over time.

　(A) suspected　　(B) summoned　　(C) supposed　　(D) sustained

(2) Disposable income is the total income someone has _____ they have paid their taxes.

　(A) before　　(B) over　　(C) under　　(D) after

(3) During a recession, unemployment rates tend to rise, and consumers tend to reduce _____.

　(A) spend　　(B) spends　　(C) spending　　(D) spent

(4) At the national level, economic resources allow countries to _____ in education, health, security, and so forth.

　(A) initiate　　(B) interact　　(C) inject　　(D) invest

Reading Activities

Read the following passage.

1 Personal wealth and income are essential aspects of living a healthy and happy life. And because our financial capacity is set by the country or region in which we live, the national or regional economy has a direct effect on our financial well-being. For example, a recession can incite a deterioration in the quality of our daily life. *Recession* is an economic term that refers to a significant decline in economic activity within a country or region. It is characterized by a sustained period of negative economic growth, typically measured by a decrease in gross domestic product (GDP) for two or more consecutive quarters or more than six months.

2 A recession can disrupt the economic stability of a country in various ways. There may be increased unemployment, reduced income, reduced consumer spending, business closures, and financial stress. Because of threats such as unemployment or reduced income, people have to be cautious and spend less money on their day-to-day needs. They look for reasonably priced daily necessities such as cheaper food, and they cut their spending on discretionary items. For example, they hesitate to spend money on dining out at restaurants, on entertainment expenses, on shopping for luxury clothing or accessories, etc. This trend usually leads to lower prices for goods and services because businesses must attract consumers who are living on a smaller budget. Although goods and services may become cheaper during a recession, this does not improve financial well-being because people still face the risks of decreased earnings and job losses.

3 When the prices of goods and services increase in a recessionary context, it is called stagflation. **[1]** It is a compound word from 'stagnation' and 'inflation.' Stagflation occurs when prices rise, the currency loses value, and there is no real growth in the economy to create jobs. **[2]** Basic necessities such as groceries, fuel, and housing become increasingly expensive. **[3]** Because people have to prioritize their expenses and adjust their lifestyles, financial well-being can be significantly undermined. **[4]**

4 Clearly, the stability of the overall economy is crucial to maintaining financial well-being. When an economy is healthy and strong, there is a much better chance for people to build wealth and attain long-term financial well-being.

aspect	側面
region	地域
direct	直接的な
recession	不景気
incite	誘因となる
deterioration	悪化
term	用語、言葉
refer to	～のこと を指す
decline	下落、減少
characterize	特徴 を示す
period	期間
typically	一般的に
measure	測定する
GDP	国内総生産
consecutive	連続した
disrupt	妨げる
business closures	廃業
cautious	用心深い
day-to-day	日々 の、毎日の
discretionary items	贅沢品
hesitate to	～する のをためらう
luxury	贅沢な
trend	傾向
attract	惹きつける
earnings	収入
context	状況
stagflation	スタグ フレーション
compound word	複合語
fuel	燃料
prioritize	優先する
adjust	調整する、 適合させる
undermine	むし ばむ
crucial	極めて重 要な
attain	実現する、達 成する

▷ Reading Comprehension 1

Read through the text and choose the correct answer.

1. What is the passage mainly about?

    a) How individual wealth affects the overall economy

    b) How a well-known company created new jobs in a recession

    c) The relationship between unemployment rates and GDP

    d) Economic factors that affect financial well-being

2. Which of the following is an example of a discretionary item?

    a) One's bank balance

    b) Spending money on a movie ticket

    c) Paying an electricity bill

    d) Disposable personal income

3. The word "deterioration" in paragraph 1, line 5, means

    a) An advance notification

    b) Something has become worse

    c) Something has been made stronger

    d) A steady development

4. In which position from **[1]** to **[4]** does the following sentence best fit?

    "As a result, our purchasing power is eroded, and we have to make difficult choices between essential items."

    a) **[1]**   b) **[2]**   c) **[3]**   d) **[4]**

▷ Reading Comprehension 2

Answer the following questions in a complete sentence.

1. What are the items that we need for our daily life called (for example, foods, clothes, household goods, and so on)?

    (called / are / necessities / they / daily)

    _____

2. Describe the word 'recession' in a single sentence using the phrase 'negative economic growth.'

    _____

Video Activities

▶▷ True or False Questions

Watch the video and check the facts. Circle T if the statement is true or F if it is false.

1. The video states that the Red Cross was originally founded in Sweden.　[T / F]
2. Marianne Örberg is working as a lawyer.　[T / F]
3. Marianne Örberg has not yet run out of her savings.　[T / F]
4. The price of basic necessities has risen very high in Stockholm.　[T / F]

▶▷ Comprehension Questions

Watch the video again and choose the correct answer. Read the script if necessary.

1. What happens when the price of basic necessities rises sharply?
   a) People have to live off their savings.
   b) People have to change their eating habits.
   c) Basic foods, like milk and eggs, will be in short supply.
   d) The number of people moving to the countryside increases.

2. Which people are likely to be the most affected by price increases?
   a) People who are granted time off work due to illness or because of other medical reasons
   b) People living in urban areas
   c) People living in the countryside
   d) People who are self-employed

3. What can you infer from the video?
   a) More than half of the Swedish population is at risk of falling into poverty.
   b) No sign of economic recovery has yet been seen.
   c) The Swedish economy is regarded as the most stable of European countries.
   d) The same recession pattern has already been observed in other European countries.

▶ Watch the video and complete the script.

In this Stockholm branch, the Red Cross collects unsold food from supermarkets and sells it on at knock down prices. Seventy-three-year-old Marianne Örberg, a pensioner and former lawyer, comes here ¹(
). She's afraid of having to use up her savings to pay for the basics.

5 **Marianne Örberg:** "Eggs, milk and butter, sour cream and yoghurt and things that you want on normal days. They are not twice as expensive but it has increased ²(   ) 50 percent for many items. People have changed their eating habits. You eat different kinds of food actually nowadays, to ³(   ). So initiatives like this are really really
10 valuable."

Martin Arnlov: "Previously we mostly saw persons living on the true margins of society, now this has changed. Also, children with families, elderly people, people who are on sick leave, all are struggling to make ends meet."

"The total number of people is still difficult to get a clear picture of if you look
15 throughout the country. And that is one area where we urge the government to make a new proper investigation on that so that we have proper facts."

The statistics paint a worrying picture. As of 2021 almost 15 percent of Swedes are at risk of falling into poverty, these are the people that are living on ⁴(   ) percent or less of the average income. And the situation might be
20 spreading across the continent.

Annika Alexius: "That figures—Sweden is the worst country in Europe. I don't, it doesn't seem that way to me. We're a little earlier than other European countries in this recession. Sweden moves more like the US in they were early with the high inflation, early with the downturn."
25 **Interviewer:** "Meaning Sweden is gonna do better at the moment when other countries are gonna do worse in the future?"
Annika Alexius: "At least they will also do worse in a while and Sweden will not be worse than other countries."

With ⁵(   ) also falling, by as much as 10 percent
30 in January alone, there are fears that this economic downturn shows no signs of easing up.

Exchanging Ideas and Thoughts

Practice the conversation with your partner. Think about how you can develop the conversation further.

A: There was a big recession in Japan when the asset 'bubble economy' burst in 1992.

B: Yes, (1) 学校で習いました _____. If there was another recession, would you change any of your spending habits?

A: Well, (2) 服のような贅沢品に使うお金を削ると思います _____
_____. How about you?

B: I think I would try to buy daily necessities at a more reasonable price by shopping around stores for the best deals.

A: That's a good idea. Using coupons at the supermarket can help save money too.

B: That's right. Actually, even though there's no recession now, it might be interesting to try to live on a stricter budget.

 ## Further Activity

(1) Visit the following website again and try using the 'Compare Your Income' web tool by the OECD to learn more about the importance of financial stability. Take notes and share some interesting figures you find with your classmates.

OECD Income (IDD) and Wealth (WDD) Distribution Databases

 https://www.oecd.org/social/income-distribution-database.htm

(2) Using key words and/or phrases you have learned from the reading and video, try Cinii Research or a similar information retrieval system to find some books and articles that are of interest to you. Compare your list of books and articles with your classmates' lists.

Unit 4 Financial Stability 3

国際情勢と経済

▼ Introduction

個人の台所事情が社会の経済状況によって左右されるように、一国の経済は国際社会全体の情勢に影響を受けます。このユニットでは、特定の地域の紛争が国際社会や世界中の人々の暮らしに与える影響について考えます。

▶ Warm Up Quizzes: Learning the Basics

Complete the sentences below and learn the basics about the international economy.

(1) Modern nations are ＿＿＿＿ interconnected through trade, finance, and global supply chains.

    (A) increased   (B) increasingly   (C) increasing   (D) increases

(2) When countries impose sanctions on other nations for political or security reasons, it can ＿＿＿＿ trade and financial flows.

    (A) disrupt   (B) disclose   (C) discover   (D) discuss

(3) The prices of ＿＿＿＿, such as oil, minerals, and agricultural products, are influenced by international events.

    (A) comrades   (B) commuters   (C) commons   (D) commodities

(4) A financial crisis in one country can quickly ＿＿＿＿ to others.

    (A) spot   (B) spoil   (C) split   (D) spread

Reading Activities

Read the following passage.

1 Individual wealth and income are heavily dependent on national and regional economic conditions. National economies and regional economic conditions are in turn impacted by global economic conditions and international events. One event that
5 has had a significant impact on the world economy in the 2020s was the Russian military invasion of Ukraine. This was not just an issue between Russia and Ukraine; several countries have since imposed economic sanctions against Russia and provided Ukraine with financial or material support. **[1]** Since Russia
10 is the second-largest supplier of natural gas, and Ukraine is one of the world's major producers of grains (such as corn and wheat), the invasion has affected the availability and purchase of these commodities. The global economy has also been impacted, and this, in turn, continues to affect the well-being of people
15 worldwide.

2 Imposing economic sanctions is a way to penalize Russia and its economy for the invasion of Ukraine. For example, sanctions have been imposed to restrict or ban the export of specific natural resources from Russia, depriving the Russian economy
20 of revenue from resources such as oil, gas, minerals, and timber. **[2]** The world economy is affected because countries that rely heavily on Russian natural resources in turn face significant challenges. They may need to diversify their resource imports, find alternative suppliers, or explore options for domestic
25 production. These adjustments can lead to higher costs, logistics problems, and the need to establish new trade relationships. Finding alternative sources or suppliers can disrupt existing supply chains and create short-term uncertainties. This can lead to price volatility and market instability, affecting both
30 industries and consumers.

3 Thousands of kilometers away from where the two countries are at war, African nations also face economic difficulties due to the invasion. The price of daily necessities such as basic groceries and diesel fuel has doubled or even tripled in Africa. **[3]** Even the
35 price of a staple food, bread, has been rising, making people's daily lives more challenging. Businesses must adjust as they try to provide goods and services under trying circumstances.

dependent on 依存している	
in turn 同様に、今度は	
military invasion 軍事侵攻	
issue 問題	
impose 課す	
economic sanction 経済制裁	
natural gas 天然ガス	
grain 穀物	
corn とうもろこし	
wheat 小麦	
commodity 商品、産物	
penalize 罰する、懲らしめる	
restrict 制限する	
ban 禁止する	
export 輸出	
specific 特定の	
natural resource 天然資源	
revenue 収益、歳入	
timber 材木	
diversify 分散する	
alternative 代替の	
explore 模索する	
logistics 物流	
volatility 変動性	
instability 不安定性、変わりやすさ	
staple food 主食	
trying 苦しい、困難な	

4 Clearly, even if individual wealth and income are stable in a certain country or region, it does not necessarily mean that financial well-being is attainable. When the cost of living increases rapidly in a short period of time, especially because
5 of an unforeseen event, it is difficult to accommodate such changes at an individual level. **[4]** People expect governments to take measures and provide financial assistance such as tax incentives, grants, or low-interest loans to overcome the economic challenges caused by international affairs. Financial well-being
10 can only be built on the secure foundations of healthy and stable national, regional and global economies.

cost of living 生活費
rapidly 急激に
unforeseen 予期しない
accommodate 受け入れる
tax incentive 税制上の優遇措置
grant 助成金

 ## Reading Comprehension 1

Read through the text and choose the correct answer.

1. Which of the following is mentioned in the first paragraph?
   a) Examples of important natural resources
   b) The historical background of the conflict between Russia and Ukraine
   c) How the global economy and individual financial well-being are connected
   d) The differences between the working of the national economy and the working of the global economy

2. What does the second paragraph describe?
   a) The kind of military support Ukraine requires
   b) How countries are providing Ukraine with financial support
   c) Why some countries are dependent on Russian natural resources
   d) Examples of the results of economic sanctions

3. The word "Businesses" in paragraph 3, line 6, means
   a) Companies   b) Financial well-being
   c) Economic sanctions   d) Military conflicts

4. In which position from **[1]** to **[4]** does the following sentence best fit?
   "These export restrictions can disrupt global supply chains."
   a) **[1]**   b) **[2]**   c) **[3]**   d) **[4]**

 ## Reading Comprehension 2

Answer the following questions in a complete sentence.

1. Why is the Russian invasion of Ukraine mentioned in the passage?
   (mentioned / as an example of / that can impact / it is / the worldwide economy / international affairs)

2. Why is the African economic situation mentioned in the passage?

_____

Video Activities

True or False Questions

Watch the video and check the facts. Circle T if the statement is true or F if it is false.

1. The story is about the development of social infrastructure in Africa.   [T / F]
2. African countries have a lot of renewable energy sources.   [T / F]
3. Economic activities in Africa heavily depend on diesel fuel.   [T / F]
4. A number of ethnic conflicts continue to hamper economic activities in   [T / F]
   Africa.

Comprehension Questions

Watch the video again and choose the correct answer. Read the script if necessary.

1. Which of the following sentences is true about the relationship between Russia and African countries?

   a) Russia has stopped importing processed food from African countries.

   b) African countries have imported grains and fertilizers from Russia.

   c) African countries are going to ban imports of wheat from Russia.

   d) Russian natural gas is the major energy source in Africa.

2. What is mentioned as one of the issues in the region?

   a) Gender inequality

   b) Underdeveloped transport infrastructure

   c) High costs of education

   d) High demand for electricity

3. What can you infer from the video?

   a) If the war in Ukraine continues, prices will rise even further.

   b) More solar panels will have to be installed to ensure a stable supply of electricity.

   c) Elementary schools will be built in rural areas.

   d) Fuel efficient trucks will be developed to improve the transportation system.

▶ Watch the video and complete the script.

From Malawi to the Maghreb, Africans are feeling the impact of the Ukraine crisis in wrenching fuel and food price increases. Global ¹( ) prices have reached a decade high since Russia invaded on February 24. In Africa, they have doubled. Nigeria subsidises petrol, but this bakery manager still pays more
5 to bake bread.

Julius Adewale: "The cost of production has increased immensely, so they have to come together now, also increased the price of bread by 40 percent to what it was before."

Meanwhile diesel and jet fuel prices are sold at market rates. Samuel Salau,
10 a construction engineer, says the price of diesel has doubled from ²( ) naira, or seventy-five dollar cents.

Samuel Salau: "Within a month it has left that level to about 600 naira something plus now. And so many industries [are] on diesel. Trucks that bring food stuff from the north to the south are running on diesel. Even trains run on
15 diesel."

In Malawi, bread is much more expensive, at this supermarket in the ³( ) Lilongwe.

Tiwonge Phakati: "It is more difficult to buy bread because the price has gone up exponentially compared to before. The amount we paid for two loaves of
20 bread is now enough only for one. We are spending more."

Both Ukraine and Russia are major suppliers of wheat and other cereals to Africa, while Russia is a key producer of fertilizer. The war and international ⁴( ) against Moscow have disrupted supply chains, up to places like Bukavu in eastern Democratic Republic of the Congo.

25 **Paulin Bishakabalya:** "We hardly produce anything and everything that is produced does not reach the market because of the state of the roads. We are totally dependent on international supplies. And the prices are going up because of the war in Ukraine. And this is reflected here in Bukavu."

This dependence has drawn concern from the UN.

30 **Antonio Guterres:** "We must do everything possible to avert a hurricane of hunger and a meltdown of the global food system."

The war has raised fears of even further increases in north Africa. Amid wholesale flour shortages, this bakery in Tunis has to buy consumer packets.

Slim Talbi: "I am buying 10 kilogrammes at 18 dinars when normally I would buy
35 50 kilogramme bag at 26 dinars. All of this before even feeling the impact of

the war. How will we work afterwards? I'm worried."

Thousands of civilians have been killed inside Ukraine. More than three million people have fled across its borders, and ⁵(   ) more are displaced inside the country. The figures are rising fast. As the conflict
5 continues, so will its impact further abroad in Africa.

Exchanging Ideas and Thoughts

Practice the conversation with your partner. Think about how you can develop the conversation further.

A: (1) 生活費は日本でも高くなってきていますね _____

_____ .

B: That's right. Groceries are more expensive, bread costs more, and restaurant prices have gone up just to give a few examples.

A: Yes. Sushi used to cost 100 yen at chain restaurants, but now you might have to pay 150 yen.

B: That's right. Cars have increased in price too. An SUV from a well-known manufacturer cost 3,620,450 yen in 2021, but the same car costs 3,925,550 yen now.

A: That's quite a jump. A lot of the price rises are connected with events and conditions in the global economy, and (2) それらが個人の経済的なウェルビーイングに影響しています

_____ .

B: I know what you mean. So do you think the situation will improve in the future?

Further Activity

1. Visit the following website to learn more about (A) the Russian military invasion of Ukraine and (B) the economic situation in Africa. Take notes and share some interesting facts and figures you find with your classmates.

United Nations, UN News

https://news.un.org/en/story/2023/03/1134122

World Bank, the World Bank in Africa

https://www.worldbank.org/en/region/afr/

2. Using key words and/or phrases you have learned from the reading and video, try Cinii Research or a similar information retrieval system to find some books and articles that are of interest to you. Compare your list of books and articles with your classmates' lists.

Unit 5 Diet and Health
食事とウェルビーイング

▼ Introduction

心身ともに健康であることが幸せな生活を送るためには重要です。そして体の健康を保つには栄養のある食事を摂ることが必要です。このユニットでは、食事の面から心と体の健康について考えるとともに、現代社会でもなくならない食糧不足の問題について知識を深めます。

▶ Warm Up Quizzes: Learning the Basics

Complete the sentences below and learn about the connection between diet and well-being.

(1) Well-balanced and nutritious meals are essential for _____ health and well-being.

   (A) maintain   (B) maintained   (C) maintaining   (D) maintenance

(2) A well-balanced meal typically _____ lean protein, whole grains, plenty of fruits and vegetables, and healthy fats.

   (A) includes   (B) including   (C) inclusion   (D) include

(3) Persistent hunger can _____ our immune system and increase susceptibility to disease.

   (A) awaken   (B) weaken   (C) darken   (D) broken

(4) Malnutrition in children can cause _____ impairment and an increased risk of long-term health problems.

   (A) cohesive   (B) cognitive   (C) coarse   (D) collective

Reading Activities

Read the following passage.

1 Healthy food is the foundation of physical well-being. A well-balanced and nourishing meal has a profound impact on our overall health and quality of life. A well-balanced meal includes a combination of proteins, carbohydrates, healthy fats, vitamins,
5 and minerals. These nutrients are essential for the growth, repair, and maintenance of our cells, tissues, and organs. Regular consumption of nutritious meals supports proper immune function, enhances metabolism, and improves the body's ability to fight off diseases and infections.

10 **2** The foods that we consume also have a direct influence on our mental and emotional well-being. They affect the production of neurotransmitters in our brain, such as serotonin and dopamine, which play a crucial role in regulating our mood, and maintaining mental clarity. Consuming a diet rich in fruits,
15 vegetables, whole grains, and lean proteins promotes brain health and has been linked to a reduced risk of mental health disorders like depression and anxiety.

3 Eating food with others also brings substantial health benefits. Having a meal with family or friends provides an opportunity for
20 social interaction and connection. It fosters a sense of community, strengthens relationships, and promotes overall happiness. **[1]** Eating together also encourages mindful eating practices, such as savoring the flavors and textures of food, which can help us develop a healthier relationship with food and prevent overeating.

25 **4** However, not everyone has access to healthy foods. Despite advances in food production, many people around the world still suffer from hunger and malnutrition. **[2]** According to the Food and Agriculture Organization (FAO), as of 2021, between 702 and 828 million people in the world have been suffering from
30 chronic lack of nutrition or hunger. Many countries in Sub-Saharan Africa, including South Sudan, Chad, Niger, and the Central African Republic, currently face high levels of food insecurity and malnutrition. Some countries in South Asia, like India, Bangladesh, and Afghanistan, struggle with high levels
35 of hunger and malnutrition. In conflict-affected regions around the world, such as Yemen, Syria, and parts of Nigeria, there is severe food insecurity and malnutrition. **[3]** This is because

foundation 基礎、土台
nourishing 栄養になる
profound 多大な
impact 影響
protein タンパク質
carbohydrate 炭水化物
nutrient 栄養素
cell 細胞
tissue 組織
organ 臓器
immune function 免疫機能
metabolism 代謝
infection 感染症
neurotransmitter 神経伝達物質
serotonin セロトニン
dopamine ドーパミン

depression 鬱
anxiety 不安
substantial 重要な、かなりの
benefit 恩恵、利点
foster 育てる、育成する

savor 味わう
flavor 味、風味
overeating 過食、食べ過ぎ

suffer from ～に苦しむ
malnutrition 栄養失調
FAO 国連食糧農業機関
chronic 慢性の、習慣的な
Sub-Saharan Africa サハラ以南のアフリカ
food insecurity 食糧不安、食糧不足
struggle with ～に苦しむ
conflict-affected region 紛争地域

armed conflicts disrupt food production, displace populations, and hamper access to humanitarian aid.

5 Meals are not merely about filling our stomachs. **[4]** They are also an essential component of our well-being. We have to be mindful of eating regular, nutritious meals and maintaining healthy eating habits. Doing so will enhance the overall quality of our own lives.

disrupt 邪魔をする、遮る
displace 立ち退かせる
humanitarian aid 人道的支援
component 構成要素

▷▷ Reading Comprehension 1

Read through the text and choose the correct answer.

1. What is NOT true about a well-balanced meal?
   a) It helps the immune system to function correctly.
   b) Regular consumption is important.
   c) It contains various nutrients.
   d) It contains neurotransmitters.

2. What can you infer from the passage?
   a) The number of people suffering from hunger cannot be measured.
   b) Food production in general has improved over the years.
   c) Hunger is currently present only in some African countries.
   d) Asian countries have better food production and food availability compared with African countries.

3. What does the passage say about depression?
   a) It is a mental health problem.
   b) It is caused by the lack of a particular nutrient.
   c) Eating with others reduces it.
   d) It hampers healthy relationships with others.

4. In which position from **[1]** to **[4]** does the following sentence best fit?
   "It allows us to engage in meaningful conversations, share experiences, and create priceless memories."
   a) **[1]**   b) **[2]**   c) **[3]**   d) **[4]**

▷▷ Reading Comprehension 2

Answer the following questions in a complete sentence.

1. Name five different nutrients of a balanced-meal in alphabetical order.

2. What can directly hamper food production in the modern world?

_____

Video Activities

 True or False Questions

Watch the video and check the facts. Circle T if the statement is true or F if it is false.

1. Two thirds of children under five are malnourished.   [T / F]

2. Nangole Lopwon works for a hospital.   [T / F]

3. Nangole's family members eat wild plants, not farm-produced crops.   [T / F]

4. Hunger can negatively affect the brain.   [T / F]

Comprehension Questions

Watch the video again and choose the correct answer. Read the script if necessary.

1. What is NOT mentioned as a cause of hunger?

a) Groups of armed robbers

b) An extended period of dry weather

c) Lack of fertilizer for crops

d) Harmful insects

2. What do you know about Nangole Lopwon?

a) Nangole is always at home taking care of her children.

b) Nangole lost one of her children due to hunger.

c) The oldest child helps Nangole with the housework every day.

d) Nangole needs to buy charcoal to do housework.

3. What measure has been introduced to help those suffering from malnutrition?

a) Carrying out group medical examinations

b) Providing free, clean water

c) Providing a free shuttle bus service to hospitals

d) Holding voluntary medical lectures

▶ Watch the video and complete the script.

The worst hunger is in Kotido, Moroto and Kaabong districts. Here, more than one child in two aged under five is badly malnourished. In district hospitals you see children half their normal weight. Their lifeline to survival is a feeding tube. Prolonged drought, waves of locusts and African army worms and predatory

5 armed groups have ravaged this impoverished area, leaving no food for people to eat.

Nangole Lopwon, a mother of six, lost her one-year-old child last year.

Nangole Lopwon: "I went to sell charcoal. And I instructed the grown child to stay with the small ones until I came back. When I came back, I found out

10 that the child was already dead. What could I do?"

The three-year-old child [1]( ) her is also malnourished.

Nangole Lopwon: "The child was not sick. It was purely the hunger that killed him. Even this one is on the brink of death."

The family's food mainly comes from wild grasses which grow nearby, but

15 which often cause diarrhea. From time to time, the family also get Plumpy'Nut—a ready-to-use therapeutic food for the malnourished.

Malnutrition can have a devastating impact on the child's long-term development.

Meri Jino: "If we don't do something right now then if they survive [2](

20), then we don't expect very good human capability, human capital in the future. Because these kids will not do well in school, they will be stunted and the development, brain and everything, will be compromised."

The situation is dire and authorities are [3]( ) to get to the grips with the scale of it all.

25 **Alex Mokori:** "In terms of acute malnutrition in this year we have experienced the worst that we have had in the last 10 years. And we are tracing this back to the issues around climate change. We have also experienced increasing pockets of insecurity as well as common childhood illnesses."

Three years into the crisis, the Ugandan Ministry of health and the local

30 authorities, supported by UNICEF, are now organizing mass screenings in the area. In this village the health workers [4]( ) malnourished children, who will now be put in special programs to help them. A week ago, this area was parched. Today it's green—a sign that even a little rain can change nature in an instant. But the problem is timing and resources. The locals say they have

35 nothing to plant now. And it's not just the [5]( ), pests and insecurity

that are causing hunger, but also the cost of food—the rapidly raising prices of commodities is increasing the numbers of hungry in this corner of Uganda. Help, say experts, is needed now.

 ## Exchanging Ideas and Thoughts

Practice the conversation with your partner. Think about how you can develop the conversation further.

A: (1) 自分の食習慣がそれほど健康的ではないことが分かりました

_____

_____.

B: Why do you say that?

A: Well, when I started university, I began living apart from my parents.

B: So you mean that it's not easy for you to prepare balanced meals?

A: Right. And I also usually eat alone. So there's no interaction at the table.

B: (2) 大学の学食でもっと一緒に昼ご飯を食べたらいいかもしれませんね

_____

_____.

 ## Further Activity

(1) Visit the following website and focus on the 'Main Topics' to learn about the FAO and its activities. Take notes and share interesting facts and figures you find with your classmates.

Food and Agriculture Organization of the United Nations, Main Topics

 https://www.fao.org/home/en

(2) Using key words and/or phrases you have learned from the reading and video, try Cinii Research or a similar information retrieval system to find some books and articles that are of interest to you. Compare your list of books and articles with your classmates' lists.

Unit 6 Health Status

医療機関の役割

▼ Introduction

健康を保つためには医療施設や医療サービスが重要な役割を果たします。このユニットでは、健康とウェルビーイングの関係とともに、社会基盤が整っていない地域での医療に関する問題について知識を深め考えます。

▶▶ Warm Up Quizzes: Learning the Basics

Complete the sentences below and learn the basics about health status in terms of well-being.

(1) Health status directly impacts physical and mental abilities _____ quality of life.

    (A) at least   (B) more or less   (C) nonetheless   (D) as well as

(2) Accessibility _____ hospital care means having timely access to emergency care, specialized medical treatments, and a comprehensive range of healthcare services.

    (A) in   (B) to   (C) for   (D) over

(3) A high quality medical service allows for timely _____ , treatment, and preventive care, contributing to better health outcomes.

    (A) diapers   (B) diary   (C) diagnosis   (D) diameter

(4) Alternative medicine often focuses _____ holistic approaches, natural remedies, and mind-body connections.

    (A) in   (B) among   (C) to   (D) on

Reading Activities

Audio 1-12

Read the following passage.

1 Achieving financial stability means that you no longer have to worry about serious financial problems such as unemployment, lack of savings, or paying off debts. However, it does not mean that your well-being is secure. Besides income and wealth, a
5 crucial factor which can enhance your well-being is health status. Health status encompasses the physical, mental, and emotional aspects of your health. When you are in good health, you have a better chance of leading a fulfilling life, of pursuing your goals, and of experiencing a higher quality of life.

10 **2** The central component of health status in terms of well-being is physical health. Being in good physical health means that you have the energy to engage in daily activities, that you have the vitality to explore the world around you, and that your body can function properly. **[1]** Good physical health is the foundation for
15 enjoying interests and physical activities, and for performing well in your personal and professional life.

3 Mental well-being is surely as important as physical health. **[2]** When mental health is compromised, it can have profound consequences on overall well-being. Good mental health promotes
20 positive emotions like happiness, contentment, and joy, while poor mental health can contribute to feelings of sadness, anxiety, irritability, and despair. Cognitive functioning, such as thinking, reasoning, problem-solving, memory, and concentration, are also affected by one's mental health status.

25 **4** In order to maintain good physical and mental health, access to healthcare facilities and medical services is crucial. In fact, healthcare facilities such as hospitals are very important for our well-being. **[3]** Immediate access to a hospital in an emergency situation is critical because every minute counts. When dealing
30 with a severe injury, a sudden illness, or a life-threatening condition, prompt medical attention can help to alleviate symptoms, prevent complications, and in some cases, save someone's life. Being in close proximity to a hospital also ensures that individuals can receive timely emergency care, minimizing
35 the risks and maximizing the chances of a positive outcome.

5 There are some factors which hamper accessibility to hospitals, such as geographic location, lack of reliable or

---

worry about 〜を心配する
debt 借金、負債
secure 心配のいらない
besides 〜の他に
enhance 高める、強める
encompass 包含する
pursue 求める、追及する

energy 精力、気力
engage 参加する
vitality 活力、活気

compromise 妥協する
consequence 結果
promote 促進する
contentment 満足感
irritability 怒りやすい性質
despair 絶望、失望
cognitive functioning 認知機能
reasoning 論理的思考
concentration 集中力
healthcare facility 医療施設
count 重要である
severe injury 重症
life-threatening 死にかかわる
prompt 迅速な、素早い
alleviate 軽減する、和らげる
complication 合併症
proximity 近いこと
minimize できる限り減らす
hamper 妨げる、妨害する
reliable 信頼性のある

affordable transportation, financial constraints, language and cultural barriers, and so forth. In Japan, where infrastructure is well developed, such negative factors may be less perceptible. [4] However, there are still many countries and regions where accessibility to hospitals is poor, and it is hard to secure a better health status.

transportation 交通手段
constraint 制約、制限

Reading Comprehension 1

Read through the text and choose the correct answer.

1. What does the passage describe?
   a) The connection between one's financial stability and health status
   b) The importance of health status and accessibility to hospitals
   c) Some examples of medical care systems around the world
   d) How someone's physical health affects their mental health

2. The word "profound" in paragraph 3, line 2, means
   a) interesting   b) painful   c) serious   d) global

3. According to the passage, which of the following would NOT affect accessibility to a hospital?
   a) Poor family bonds   b) Lack of basic literacy skills
   c) Remoteness   d) Not owning a car or motorbike

4. In which position from [1] to [4] does the following sentence best fit?
   "It affects how we think, feel, and act in our daily life."
   a) [1]   b) [2]   c) [3]   d) [4]

Reading Comprehension 2

Answer the following questions in a complete sentence.

1. Describe how poor mental health affects us.
   (and impairs / contributes to / it / cognitive-functioning / mental instability)

_____

2. How does proximity to a hospital enhance positive medical outcomes?

_____

 **Video Activities**

▶▷ True or False Questions

Watch the video and check the facts. Circle T if the statement is true or F if it is false.

1. The story is from India.   [T / F]
2. It is mainly about a volunteer activity at a soup kitchen.   [T / F]
3. Doctors in the video are not officially certified medical doctors.   [T / F]
4. Some people believe in folk remedies.   [T / F]

▶▷ Comprehension Questions

Watch the video again and choose the correct answer. Read the script if necessary.

1. Which of the following is true about issues in Naga territory?

    a) Social infrastructure in the region is very poor.

    b) Teenagers in the region do not have a chance to receive higher education.

    c) The region has been suffering from ethnic conflicts for years.

    d) High crime rates in the region have been getting attention.

2. What do you know about Mg Taing Khite?

    a) He is a volunteer trainee.

    b) He is a villager in medical need.

    c) He is a staff member of an NGO.

    d) He is the reporter of the story.

3. What can you infer from the video?

    a) Bringing modern medicine to remote areas is a key activity of the NGO.

    b) Medical volunteer activities have been established by the local government.

    c) The mobile clinic in the video is managed by only one medical doctor.

    d) Protecting cultural customs is the key to providing successful medical services.

▶▶ Watch the video and complete the script.

 🔊 Audio 1-13

All in a day's commute for these daring doctors in Myanmar's far north. This is Naga territory, a tribal region of former headhunters near the Indian border. Isolated from the ¹( ) of the country, it's desperately under-developed.

5

Dr. Zaw Min Lay: "Language, transportation and zero telecommunication are the major challenges we're facing."

10 His teams go village-to-village, giving health education ²( ) and opening mobile clinics that run long into the night. Mg Taing Khite has rickets a disease that results in weak bones and ³( ) walk just a couple of months ago. After a course of vitamin D and calcium, the six-year-old's on the mend. The NGO also helps get emergency cases to hospital, 15 often several days' walk away.

Mg's father: "We have no motorbikes and no money to pay for a motorbike taxi to get to the hospital. As farmers, we have many things to do."

Crucially, the medical teams are also training up a volunteer in each of the region's ⁴( ) villages. The trainees give out basic medicines, screen for TB* 20 and carry out on-the-spot malaria tests. Htan Pi's been a volunteer for nearly three years. But her family's been in the healing business for generations. Her mother is the village shaman.

Htan Pi: "People normally come to me first. I give medicines to them and they only go to my mum if they don't get better."

25 One example, her mum says, was a man whose severe swelling wasn't going down in hospital.

Jang Ngon: "We needed to call his soul back from the jungle. So we sacrificed a chicken and the patient got better."

Changing habits might ⁵( ). But the volunteers are helping 30 bring modern medicine to this remote region, bridging the healthcare gap thanks to their band of mentors on motorbikes.

*tuberculosisの略。「結核」。

Exchanging Ideas and Thoughts

Practice the conversation with your partner. Think about how you can develop the conversation further.

A: I kind of worry about my physical health. With so much homework to do, (1) 運動する時間があまりありません _____ .

B: I know what you mean. (2)ヨガをやってみようと思ったことはないですか _____ ? It's good for physical and mental health.

A: Oh, that's a good idea. How does Yoga help with your health?

B: Well, it helps me to stay positive, and I feel energized after each class. I recommend giving it a try.

A: Actually, I'd like to. Maybe I can come with you to Yoga class one day?

B: Sure. As students, it's really important to look after our physical and mental health.

 **Further Activity**

(1) Visit the following website to learn more about accessibility to hospitals. Take notes and share some interesting facts and figures that you find with your classmates.

UNHCR The UN Refugee Agency, Access to Healthcare

 https://www.unhcr.org/what-we-do/protect-human-rights/public-health/access-healthcare

(2) Using key words and/or phrases you have learned from the reading and video, try Cinii Research or a similar information retrieval system to find some books and articles that are of interest to you. Compare your list of books and articles with your classmates' lists.

Unit 7 Mental Health
アニマルセラピー

▼ Introduction

体の健康と同様に心の健康もウェルビーイングには大切です。このユニットではメンタルヘルスに注目し、現代人が陥りやすい心の問題とアニマルセラピーの実例について学びます。

▶▶ Warm Up Quizzes: Learning the Basics

Complete the sentences below and learn the basics about mental health in terms of well-being.

(1) Mental health _____ emotional stability, cognitive functioning, relationships, self-esteem, and your overall quality of life.

   (A) influence   (B) to be influenced (C) influencing   (D) influences

(2) Mental health issues _____ anxiety disorders, depression, insomnia, eating disorders, phobias, social anxiety, and so on.

   (A) include   (B) includes   (C) including   (D) to be included

(3) Someone's mental health issues, _____ chronic stress and emotional distress, can influence physical health.

   (A) as long as   (B) at least   (C) such as   (D) up to

(4) There are various types of therapy _____ to address mental health concerns.

   (A) arbitrary   (B) available   (C) aesthetic   (D) associate

🪷 Reading Activities

Read the following passage.

1 To promote and maintain mental well-being, therapy plays an important role. It is an invaluable resource to help people who are facing a wide range of challenges, from everyday stressors to more complex mental health conditions.

5 **2** There are many reasons why having therapy can be worthwhile. First, therapy provides a safe and supportive environment where individuals in need can openly express their thoughts, feelings, and concerns. **[1]** Second, through conversations with a therapist, individuals can gain a deeper understanding of their
10 emotions, thoughts, and patterns of behavior. This self-awareness allows them to identify and address underlying issues to make positive changes in their lives. **[2]** Third, therapists equip individuals with a variety of coping skills to manage stress, regulate emotions, and navigate life's challenges effectively.
15 They provide practical tools, techniques, and strategies tailored to an individual's specific needs. Therapy helps people to build resilience, enabling them to bounce back from setbacks and adapt to change with greater ease. **[3]** Fourth, therapy provides individuals with the necessary tools and support to cope with
20 symptoms, reduce distress, and enhance overall functioning for better mental health management. Fifth, therapy offers effective strategies for managing stress and enhancing overall well-being. We can learn relaxation techniques, mindfulness practices, and stress management skills. **[4]** By addressing underlying issues
25 contributing to stress, therapy helps individuals lead a more balanced and fulfilling life.

3 There are many effective forms of therapy, such as Cognitive Behavioral Therapy (CBT), Psychoanalysis Therapy, Humanistic Therapy, and Dialectical Behavior Therapy (DBT), but animal
30 therapy in particular has been recognized for its significant contributions to better mental well-being. Animal therapy, also known as animal-assisted therapy or AAT, is a type of therapy that involves meeting and connecting with animals to promote emotional, physical, and mental well-being. Some of the main
35 forms of animal therapy are Equine Therapy, Canine Therapy, Dolphin Therapy, and Feline Therapy.

4 Animals often act as social catalysts, facilitating interactions

---

role 役割
invaluable 貴重な、非常に有益な
resource 方策
stressor ストレス要因、ストレッサー
complex 複雑な、入り組んだ
worthwhile 価値のある
supportive やさしく接する、協力的な
in need 困っている、助けを必要としている
self-awareness 自己認識
identify 特定する、認識する
underlying 根本的な
coping skill 対処能力
regulate 整える、調整する
navigate 乗り越える
tailored to ～に合わせてある
resilience 回復力、立ち直る力
bounce back 元気を取り戻す
relaxation technique 緊張や不安を和らげる方法
mindfulness マインドフルネス
CBT 認知行動療法
Psychoanalysis Therapy 精神分析的心理療法
Humanistic Therapy 人間性心理療法
DBT 弁証法的行動療法
equine 馬の
canine 犬の
feline 猫の
catalyst 触媒 (変化や刺激を与えるもの)
facilitate 容易にする、促進する

between humans. Therapy animals can help to break down social barriers, encourage communication, and create a sense of belonging between people. This is especially valuable for individuals with social anxiety, autism spectrum disorder, or other conditions that hinder social engagement. Some people feel more comfortable with therapy animals than therapists. When people face diversifying stressors, animal therapy has been shown to make a strong and positive contribution to improving mental health.

social anxiety　社会不安症
autism spectrum disorder　自閉スペクトラム症
hinder　妨げる
diversifying　多様化する

 ## Reading Comprehension 1

Read through the text and choose the correct answer.

1. What is the passage mainly about?
   a) The importance of therapy for our mental health
   b) The qualifications needed to be a professional therapist
   c) Major medicines used to treat mental issues
   d) The history of animal therapy

2. How many varieties of animal therapies are introduced in the passage?
   a) Three　　b) Four　　c) Five　　d) Nine

3. The phrase "coping skills" in paragraph 2, line 9, means
   a) Techniques to deal with certain mental health issues
   b) Technologies that are utilized in medical services
   c) Institutions for people with mental problems
   d) Physical toughness

4. In which position from **[1]** to **[4]** does the following sentence best fit?
   "Having a non-judgmental and empathetic professional to talk to can lighten an individual's sense of emotional burden."
   a) **[1]**　　b) **[2]**　　c) **[3]**　　d) **[4]**

 ## Reading Comprehension 2

Answer the following questions in a complete sentence.

1. What kind of environment does therapy provide?
   (safe / environment / a / and supportive / it provides)

2. How do therapy animals help people with mental health issues?

 **Video Activities**

▶▷ **True or False Questions**

Watch the video and check the facts. Circle T if the statement is true or F if it is false.

1. Students attend the institution everyday. [T / F]
2. The institution is designed for students under 15 years old. [T / F]
3. Students at the institution aim to become professional jockeys. [T / F]
4. Horses are called 'gentle giants' in the video. [T / F]

▶▷ **Comprehension Questions**

Watch the video again and choose the correct answer. Read the script if necessary.

1. What does the video tell you about racehorses?
   a) They have retired and are learning to slow down.
   b) The are young, and they can run very fast.
   c) Special training is required to be a racehorse.
   d) The number of racehorses at the institution has been decreasing.

2. What sort of process functions as therapy?
   a) Observing how horses communicate with each other.
   b) Learning how to ride a horse.
   c) Studying to be a professional jockey.
   d) Building relationships with horses.

3. What can you infer from the video?
   a) The institution gets grants from the local government.
   b) The institution exists not only to help people with mental issues but also to take care of retired horses.
   c) The number of students at the institution has been increasing over the years.
   d) The institution was originally established to help students suffering from financial problems.

Shaun is ¹(   ) retired racehorses and they're also looking after him. The 15-year-old has Asperger's Syndrome and anger

5 ²(   ), but his equine friends have a profoundly calming influence.

Shaun: "If you're happy, they're happy. They follow what you are feeling which is really helpful, so if you're

10   feeling sad they will try and make you a little bit happier and keep you in peace."

Greatwood, in the Wiltshire countryside, was ³(   ) as a home for retired racehorses 24 years ago. It has since been transformed into a place that helps children with special educational ⁴(   ). Students, often from

15 troubled backgrounds, attend once a week on courses that are part of the school term.

Sasha Thorbek-Hooper: "Some of the learners that come to us have difficulty in building relationships with their peers and humans. And they, as we do, as humans gravitate towards certain personalities of people, and the horses

20   have personalities and the young people will gravitate towards a horse of a personality that fits with them. So it's... and that helps them when they go back in their mainstream life and school."

Another goal of Greatwood is to find the horses a long-term home. Trainer James is working with Quick Touch, a recent arrival from the track in Dubai.

25 Like most thoroughbred racehorses he can be highly-strung, but he's being taught to put his competitive instincts aside and ⁵(   ) a slower pace of life.

James Taylor: "They're taught just to go and race and that's all they know. They don't know anything else. They're straight out the gallops. And the way you ride a racehorse is when you want them to go faster, you squeeze the

30   reins and they don't come off the leg, you squeeze harder. We do exactly the opposite. We try to bring them in and teach them just to relax a bit more and have softer mouths."

Former students at Greatwood have gone on to work in stableyards or as jockeys. But even if they don't end up with equestrian careers, time spent with

35 these gentle giants will often add a touch of peace to complicated daily life.

Exchanging Ideas and Thoughts

Practice the conversation with your partner. Think about how you can develop the conversation further.

A: (1) そんなに多くの種類のアニマルセラピーがあるのは知りませんでした

_____

_____.

B: Me neither. And I was interested to learn that if you are angry or very sad, interacting with animals such as horses can help to calm your feelings.

A: That's right. I have a pet dog, and actually, when I take it for a walk, I do feel calmer.

B: I see. I've never had a pet, so the idea of animal therapy is really quite new to me.

A: Which kind of animal therapy are you most interested in?

B: (2) ドルフィンセラピーに一番興味があります _____

_____. Dolphins are very social and intelligent, so I imagine they would be ideal for animal therapy.

Further Activity

(1) Visit the following website and focus on the 'Fact sheets' to learn more about mental health-related issues. Take notes and share some interesting facts and figures you find with your classmates.

WHO, Mental health

   https://www.who.int/health-topics/mental-health#tab=tab_1

(2) Using key words and/or phrases you have learned from the reading and video, try Cinii Research or a similar information retrieval system to find some books and articles that are of interest to you. Compare your list of books and articles with your classmates' lists.

Unit 8 Housing Conditions
住宅を考える

▼ Introduction

快適な生活を送るには設備が整った住宅が必要です。このユニットでは、これからの住宅のための技術発展について知識を深めるとともに、現代社会が抱える住宅に関する課題について考えます。

▶▶ Warm Up Quizzes: Learning the Basics

Complete the sentences below and learn about issues related to housing conditions.

(1) *Housing conditions* refer to the state or quality of a _____ space.

    (A) life   (B) live   (C) living   (D) lived

(2) Housing conditions can impact the _____, safety, and overall well-being of individuals or families.

    (A) competitor   (B) complex   (C) comfort   (D) composition

(3) Good housing conditions are essential for people's health and _____ childhood development.

    (A) affect   (B) affirm   (C) afflict   (D) affix

(4) The cost of a home constitutes the main component of household _____.

    (A) wealth   (B) willpower   (C) warmth   (D) warehouse

🪷 Reading Activities

Read the following passage.

1 Housing is vital in terms of our overall well-being. It is more than just a shelter because it is deeply intertwined with people's physical, mental, and social well-being. Adequate housing is a fundamental human need and is widely recognized as one of the
5 essential determinants of health and quality of life.

2 To begin with, a sense of safety and protection is one of the most important components provided by a stable housing environment. **[1]** Having a secure place to call home fosters peace of mind and enables people to focus on other aspects of their lives, such as
10 work, education, and relationships. Also, housing conditions are crucial from the viewpoint of physical health. **[2]** Access to clean water, sanitation facilities, and proper ventilation are essential for preventing the spread of diseases and maintaining good health. Inadequate housing, on the other hand, can contribute to the
15 development or exacerbation of health issues such as respiratory illnesses, allergies, and mental health conditions. Another point housing contributes to is child development. **[3]** Suitable housing is particularly vital for children's well-being and development. A stable home environment supports their physical, cognitive,
20 and emotional growth. Children living in a safe and nurturing home environment are more likely to have better educational outcomes and experience less exposure to violence. They also have improved social connections. All of these points contribute to children's overall well-being and future success. Finally,
25 having a secure and stable home enables people to plan for the future and invest in their long-term goals. **[4]** Housing stability also has a positive impact on social mobility, reducing poverty, and breaking the cycle of disadvantage.

3 Since housing conditions play such an essential role in
30 enhancing our overall well-being, it is important to develop technologies that can improve housing conditions. There are now research facilities and programs which can assess the energy efficiency of buildings and develop innovative solutions for reducing energy consumption. Energy House 2, for example, is a
35 research facility based at the University of Salford in England. It is a full-scale, environmentally controlled house that replicates real-world conditions to evaluate the energy performance of

vital 極めて重要な	
shelter （最低限の）住まい	
intertwine 絡み合う	
adequate 十分な	
sense of safety 安心感	
stable 安定した	
secure 安全な、しっかりした	
foster 育てる	
enable できるようにする	
sanitation facility 衛生設備	
ventilation 換気	
inadequate 不十分な	
exacerbation 悪化	
respiratory 呼吸器系の	
allergy アレルギー	
cognitive 認知の	
nurturing 子育ての、子供を大切にする	
outcome 成果	
exposure さらされること	
invest in ～に投資する	
social mobility 社会的流動性	
energy efficiency エネルギー効率	
innovative 革新的な	
solution 問題解決策	
consumption 消費	

buildings. The facility allows researchers to investigate and assess building materials, insulation methods, and energy-saving technologies. Findings from such research will surely contribute to the creation of better housing for future societies.

investigate 調査する
building materials 建築資材
insulation 断熱

 Reading Comprehension 1

Read through the text and choose the correct answer.

1. Which of the following is NOT mentioned as a component that good housing can provide?

   a) Staying in good physical health   b) Developing our social status

   c) Feeling a sense of safety   d) Children's welfare

2. According to the passage, what health issue could poor housing conditions cause?

   a) Allergies   b) Fevers

   c) Headaches   d) Diarrhea

3. The word "replicates" in paragraph 3, line 8, means

   a) To watch carefully

   b) To gain knowledge about something

   c) To make an exact copy of something

   d) To purchase something expensive

4. In which position from **[1]** to **[4]** does the following sentence best fit?

   "It allows us to focus on personal development, career advancement, and building strong relationships."

   a) **[1]**   b) **[2]**   c) **[3]**   d) **[4]**

 Reading Comprehension 2

Answer the following questions in a complete sentence.

1. How do housing conditions affect education for children?
   (proper housing / educational outcomes / living in / children / better / tend to have).

   _____

2. Describe 'Energy House 2' in a single sentence.

   _____

 **Video Activities**

 True or False Questions

Watch the video and check the facts. Circle T if the statement is true or F if it is false.

1. The video is about how to get a mortgage in England. [T / F]
2. The video explains some problems caused by snowfall. [T / F]
3. Some people will actually live in an experimental house for research purposes. [T / F]
4. Energy House 2 is introduced as one of the most expensive research facilities in the world. [T / F]

▶▷ Comprehension Questions

Watch the video again and choose the correct answer. Read the script if necessary.

1. What does the video tell you about Energy House 2?
   a) Researchers can control the weather in the chambers.
   b) It is in England but was founded by a foreign company.
   c) It was built in order to develop efficient home appliances.
   d) Houses in the research chambers do not look like an ordinary house.

2. What is one of the advantages of Energy House 2?
   a) Thanks to a government grant, researchers do not have to worry about expenses.
   b) Public transportation to the facility is very convenient.
   c) Expenses for research activities can be greatly reduced.
   d) Researchers can obtain data in a relatively short period of time.

3. What can you infer from the video?
   a) It is against research ethics to develop profit-oriented research projects.
   b) More research projects should be financially supported by the government.
   c) Energy efficiency is crucial in modern society.
   d) Collaboration between industry and universities is the key to creating successful research projects.

▶ Watch the video and complete the script.

It's a ¹(   ) minus 10 Celsius here on this street in Salford, in the north of England. But it's about to get even colder, as someone's switched on a snow machine. This is clearly no ordinary neighborhood. ²(   ), we're inside a giant new facility designed to put energy efficient homes through their
5 paces.

Prof. Will Swan: "So, welcome to Energy House 2."

Professor Will Swan is the mega-lab's director.

Prof. Will Swan: "When you try and understand, you know, how a house is energy
efficient, you normally have to wait for the weather. So here we bring the
10   weather to the research problem. We can compress a two-year experiment
into sometimes a matter of weeks."

These prototype homes have been built inside one of the lab's two massive chambers. The scientists here can literally change the weather—adding wind, rain, snow or sunshine, in temperatures from minus 20 to plus 40 degrees all
15 from the comfort of their ³(   ) control room.

Prof. Will Swan: "What we're experimenting on is everything. So doors, windows,
insulation, fabric, right the way down to the heating and cooling systems we
need in the homes. The experiments we're doing here now with our partners
are really to try and understand how we deliver those future net zero homes
20   in the UK."

The test homes themselves are made by some of Britain's biggest house builders, so they don't stand out. But look closer and you'll start noticing innovative features.

Tom Cox: "We've got the panel heating, which is a point source in the room. And
25   then we've got a very unique research product up here which is an infra-red
coving."

Mirrors also act as infra-red radiators, sensors monitor which rooms are
⁴(   ), and air-source heat pumps are being tested. That's a lot of tech—and
a key challenge is how to make sure it all work together ⁵(   ).

30 **Tom Cox:** "So one of the key technologies which we're trying on this house is
almost like a building management system for residential buildings. You
connect all of that technology into a single interface. It's almost like the
Alexa of the home energy system and that can be automated as much as the
occupant wants."

35   To ensure this works in real-world conditions, volunteers are actually going

to live here for days at a time. Different structures will also be built here in the coming years, allowing homes from around the world to be tested in their own climate conditions.

5   With Russia's invasion of Ukraine raising prices, and energy efficiency crucial to fighting climate change, the team behind Energy House 2 hope their lab will help shape the future of how we live.

Exchanging Ideas and Thoughts

Practice the conversation with your partner. Think about how you can develop the conversation further.

A: (1)居住環境についてあまり考えたことはありませんでした _____

_____, but after doing this

unit I feel like I should appreciate my own home a lot more.

B: Yeah, I know what you mean. (2) 親と同居してるんですか _____

_____?

A: Yes, I do. And I have my own bedroom, so it's pretty comfortable.

B: Nice! I like my home too, but it does get cold in winter. So I am interested in how energy efficiency will improve in future houses, especially for heating.

A: Right. And if utility costs like heating could be reduced because of improvements in building technologies, that would be good for everyone.

B: Yes, it would. It would save everyone some money. But right now, I can't imagine looking for a home with good energy efficiency. It's something I'll think about in the future.

Further Activity

(1) Visit the following website to learn more about the Energy House 2 project. Take notes and share some interesting facts and figures you find with your classmates.

University of Salford, Energy House 2.0 project

https://energyhouse2.salford.ac.uk/

(2) Using key words and/or phrases you have learned from the reading and video, try Cinii Research or a similar information retrieval system to find some books and articles that are of interest to you. Compare your list of books and articles with your classmates' lists.

Unit 9 Homelessness
ホームレス問題

▼ Introduction

住居の重要性とこれからの居住環境をよりよくしていくための試みについては Unit 8 で学びました。一方で、世界には設備の整った住居での暮らしができない人たちも多くいます。このユニットでは現代社会が抱えるホームレス問題について考えます。

▶▶ Warm Up Quizzes: Learning the Basics

Complete the sentences below and learn about how homelessness affects well-being.

(1) Homelessness refers to the condition of individuals or families _____ a stable, safe, and adequate place to live.

   (A) lack   (B) lacks   (C) lacked   (D) lacking

(2) Homelessness often results _____ a combination of economic, social, and personal factors.

   (A) from   (B) between   (C) among   (D) toward

(3) Homeless people have to face various issues such as lack of stable housing, _____ access to healthcare and social services, and food insecurity.

   (A) limit   (B) limited   (C) limits   (D) limiting

(4) It is said that _____, an estimated 150 million people are homeless.

   (A) gently   (B) geographically   (C) greatly   (D) globally

Reading Activities

🔊 Audio 2-01

Read the following passage.

1 Since housing is a very important part of living a stable life, the lack of a fixed, regular, and secure nighttime residence can have a serious impact on well-being. For instance, when individuals do not have a fixed permanent address, they often face severe
5 challenges in accessing official benefits like healthcare. This is because many official documents, applications, and services require a valid address for identification and communication purposes. Without access to healthcare, people are left untreated and cannot manage their health conditions properly. In addition,
10 lack of shelter, exposure to harsh weather conditions, and limited access to nutritious food can result in malnutrition, chronic illnesses, infections, and physical injuries. The constant struggle to meet basic needs can also contribute to fatigue, sleep deprivation, and a weakened immune system. **[1]**

15 **2** Homelessness affects not only one's physical well-being but also one's mental health. The experience of homelessness can be traumatic and stressful, leading to increased rates of depression, anxiety, post-traumatic stress disorder (PTSD), and substance abuse. The lack of stability, social support, and a sense of belonging
20 can further exacerbate these mental health challenges. **[2]**.

3 Social isolation and exclusion from mainstream society is another serious problem caused by homelessness. The loss of a stable home and community connections can result in the breakdown of social networks, leading to feelings of loneliness,
25 alienation, and a loss of identity. The stigma associated with homelessness can also contribute to further isolation, as individuals may face discrimination and prejudice, making it difficult to establish new relationships or even reintegrate into society. **[3]**

30 **4** Some people assume that homelessness is most serious in developing countries with poor social infrastructure, but homelessness is also a serious problem in developed countries. Countries such as the United States, Canada, and Australia have substantial homeless populations. In Australia, for instance,
35 according to the Australian Bureau of Statistics, an estimated 116,000 people experience homelessness on any given night. The high cost of housing, unemployment, domestic violence,

fixed 決まった	
nighttime residence 寝泊りできる場所	
permanent address 低住所、本籍地	
severe 深刻な	
healthcare 医療	
require 必要とする、要求する	
valid 有効な	
identification 本人確認	
harsh 厳しい	
nutritious 栄養のある	
result in ～という結果になる	
malnutrition 栄養失調	
infection 感染症	
injury けが	
constant 絶えず続く	
fatigue 疲労、倦怠感	
sleep deprivation 睡眠不足	
immune system 免疫系	
traumatic 精神的な痛手	
PTSD 心的外傷後ストレス障害	
substance abuse 薬物乱用	
exacerbate 悪化させる、悪くする	
exclusion 排除、除外	
alienation 疎外感	
stigma 汚名、烙印	
discrimination 差別	
prejudice 偏見	
reintegrate 復帰する	
social infrastructure 社会基盤	
substantial 相当な、かなりの	
estimated 推定	

mental health issues, and substance abuse all contribute to the severity of the issue. Efforts to address homelessness require a comprehensive approach involving housing policies, social support systems, mental health services, and poverty alleviation
5 strategies. **[4]**

severity 重大性、過酷さ
comprehensive 包括的な
alleviation 緩和、削減

 ## Reading Comprehension 1

Read through the text and choose the correct answer.

1. What is the passage mainly about?
   a) The impact of homelessness on physical and mental health
   b) The experiences of homeless people in urban areas
   c) The issue of homelessness in developing countries
   d) The availability of public services providing support to homeless people

2. According to the text, which of the following problems affects homeless people?
   a) Overeating   b) Lack of sleep
   c) Learning disorders   d) Lack of exercise

3. The word "shelter" in paragraph 1, line 10, means
   a) a public service   b) an activity by an NGO
   c) a residence   d) a social network

4. In which position from **[1]** to **[4]** does the following sentence best fit?
   "Statistically, homeless individuals are also at a higher risk of suicide compared to the general population."
   a) **[1]**   b) **[2]**   c) **[3]**   d) **[4]**

 ## Reading Comprehension 2

Answer the following questions in a complete sentence.

1. Why are some countries mentioned in the last paragraph?
   (homelessness / a serious issue / they are / is / in / mentioned / developed countries / because)

   _____

2. What do you think is the most serious problem caused by homelessness?

   _____

Video Activities

▶▷ True or False Questions

Watch the video and check the facts. Circle T if the statement is true or F if it is false.

1. The story is about a recession in Australia.   [T / F]
2. Australia is known for having an unstable economy.   [T / F]
3. The economy in Australia is generally quite strong.   [T / F]
4. There was a financial crisis in Australia about six months ago. [T / F]

▶▷ Comprehension Questions

Watch the video again and choose the correct answer. Read the script if necessary.

1. What does the report tell you about homelessness in Australia?
   a) There are plenty of shelters for the homeless.
   b) Most cases of homelessness in Australia have little to do with Australia's economic conditions.
   c) There are not so many homeless people, but many Australians are facing financial problems.
   d) The number of people in need has been increasing.

2. What issue is described as the main cause of homelessness in the video?
   a) Lack of affordable housing
   b) Excessive investment in the stock market
   c) A decrease in the number of welfare programs in major cities
   d) High unemployment rates

3. What can you infer from the video?
   a) Homelessness can occur even when the economy is booming.
   b) Recession is one of the key factors that cause homelessness.
   c) The definition of homelessness differs from country to country.
   d) Welfare agencies in Australia provide lectures about homelessness.

▶▶ Watch the video and complete the script.

One of the world's richest countries with a ¹( ) beating economy. Australia has undergone ²( ) years without a recession. But not everyone
5 has benefited from the ³( ) which has seen property prices surge beyond the reach of many.

Chad Magee: "I came here six months ago, about six months ago, five-six
10 months ago, about five-six months ago and that was a humbling experience."

Experts warn that homelessness is ⁴( ) and the
15 number of people seeking help is at never seen-before levels.

Katherine McKernan: "In Sydney for example, in New South Wales, there's a ⁵( )-strong waiting list for social housing. And the private rental market is just really unaffordable for people on income support."

20 Lanz Priestley set up the Martin Place "safe space" in the heart of Sydney's CBD*. He offers the homeless shelter and free food around-the-clock.

Lanz Priestley: "People have the basic
25 human right to be safe. And if they don't have the ability to provide for their safety, and we can, then we must."

With property prices still on the rise, the government is facing a warning
30 from welfare agencies: provide more affordable housing or risk more Australians sleeping rough.

*CBD: Central Business District の略。「ビジネス中心区域」の意。

Exchanging Ideas and Thoughts

Practice the conversation with your partner. Think about how you can develop the conversation further.

A: I didn't realize that many people are at risk of being homeless.

B: Yes, and even if the economy is strong, if you lose your job or if housing is very expensive, you can be pushed into homelessness.

A: Right. In the video, the reporter mentioned that (1) 手の届く住宅がホームレスを減らすには非常に重要です _____
_____. Do you agree?

B: Yes, I do. Because if housing is very expensive, then people can't make enough money to pay rent, and they will simply lose their home.

A: Yes, and with no home it becomes more difficult to apply for a new job or take care of your health.

B: Right. And (2) 路上で生活するのは安全ではありません _____
_____. Homelessness brings so many additional problems that it is better to avoid it in the first place.

 **Further Activity**

(1) Visit the following website to learn more about homeless-related issues. Take notes and share interesting some facts and figures you find with your classmates.

United Nations, Homelessness and human rights

 https://www.ohchr.org/en/special-procedures/sr-housing/homelessness-and-human-rights

(2) Using key words and/or phrases you have learned from the reading and video, try Cinii Research or a similar information retrieval system to find some books and articles that are of interest to you. Compare your list of books and articles with your classmates' lists.

Civic Engagement

社会との関わり方

▼ Introduction

私たちの一人ひとりの暮らしは、コミュニティーとの関わりなしには語ることができません。このユニットでは、ウェルビーイングの観点から市民参加について考え、選挙の事例について学びます。

▶ Warm Up Quizzes: Learning the Basics

Complete the sentences below and learn the basics about civic engagement.

(1) Civic engagement refers to the various activities that people perform to express their political _____ and contribute to the political functioning of society.

    (A) vessel   (B) value   (C) voice   (D) vitality

(2) Political voice refers to the ability to _____ one's opinions, concerns, and demands within the political system and influence decision-making processes.

    (A) express   (B) expire   (C) expand   (D) expend

(3) Civic engagement allows individuals to develop a sense of _____ to their community.

    (A) belong   (B) belongs   (C) belonged   (D) belonging

(4) By _____ in political activities, people openly express their preferences and needs.

    (A) engage   (B) engages   (C) engaged   (D) engaging

Reading Activities

🔊 Audio 2-03

Read the following passage.

1 'No man is an island' is a well-known saying, and it means that we cannot live life detached from other people. In fact, to some extent, quality of life depends on our level of social engagement, so participating in democratic processes and activities that
5 contribute to the betterment of society is very important. One key aspect of civic engagement is that it fosters a sense of belonging and connectedness. When we actively participate in our communities, whether through volunteering, joining local organizations, or participating in public meetings, we develop a
10 deeper connection to our surroundings and the people around them. **[1]** This sense of belonging not only enhances social cohesion but also promotes mental and emotional well-being by reducing feelings of isolation and loneliness.

2 Civic engagement is also empowering because it allows us to
15 exercise our voice and take greater control over our own lives. By participating in democratic processes such as voting, attending public hearings, or contacting elected officials, we can advocate for our own interests and values. **[2]** Active participation in democracy increases our sense of agency and enhances our sense
20 of well-being and satisfaction.

3 While civic engagement has numerous benefits on well-being, there are certain barriers and challenges that can hinder individuals' involvement in civic activities. One of the main barriers to civic engagement is a simple lack of awareness of
25 the opportunities to engage in political processes. People may be unaware of local organizations, community events, or how to effectively participate in decision-making processes. **[3]** A simple lack of knowledge of how to participate in civic affairs can be enough to stop individuals from getting involved, and this means
30 that the benefits of civic engagement on well-being are never realized.

4 Another possible barrier to participating in civic activities is disillusionment. Disillusionment with the political system and a perception of its ineffectiveness can lead to apathy and
35 disengagement. Negative experiences or a lack of trust in institutions and their leaders can erode individuals' motivation to participate in civic activities. **[4]** When we feel that our voices

---

No man is an island.「人間は一人では生きられない」（17世紀の詩人ジョン・ダンによることわざ）
saying ことわざ
detached from 〜から切り離して
to some extent ある程度は
participate in 参加する
democratic 民主的な
betterment 向上、改善
connectedness つながり
surroundings 周囲
cohesion まとまり、団結
promote 促進する
isolation 孤立
empower 力を与える、できるようにする
voting 投票
public hearing 公聴会
elected official 選挙で選ばれた政治家
advocate 主張する
sense of agency 行為主体性の感覚
numerous 多くの、数々の
barrier 障害、障壁
hinder 妨げる
involvement 関わり
awareness 気づき
political process 政治過程、政治的プロセス

realize 実現する
perception 認識
ineffectiveness 効果のなさ、むだなこと
lead to 〜につながる
apathy 無関心
disengagement 離脱、撤退
erode 侵食する

are not heard or that our actions have little impact, our well-being may be adversely affected, leading to a sense of powerlessness and disconnection.

5 There are other factors that hamper civic engagement, such as restrictions on political freedoms, repressive legal frameworks, internet and media restrictions, and ethnic tensions and conflicts. To help build open and inclusive political spaces and to protect fundamental human rights, the strengthening of democratic institutions and the safeguarding of freedom of expression is required.

adversely 逆に
powerlessness 無力感、無力であること
restriction 制限、制約
repressive 弾圧的な、圧制的な
ethnic 民族の
conflict 紛争
inclusive 包括的な
safeguard 守る、保護する

 ## Reading Comprehension 1

Read through the text and choose the correct answer.

1. The phrase "a sense of belonging" in paragraph 1, lines 6-7, means
   a) Understanding the social norms of a community
   b) Receiving welfare assistance in a community
   c) Feeling accepted into a community as a valuable member
   d) Following the rules and regulations of a community

2. What is NOT an example of civic engagement?
   a) Installing a security system in a house
   b) Engaging in a cleanup activity as a volunteer member
   c) Participating in an election
   d) Attending a meeting for a neighborhood association

3. The word "disillusionment" in paragraph 4, line 2, means
   a) a feeling of disappointment   b) an unforeseen event
   c) a complicated system or structure   d) critical thinking

4. In which position from **[1]** to **[4]** does the following sentence best fit?
   "Having a say in decision-making processes that impact our communities provides a sense of empowerment and control over one's life."
   a) **[1]**   b) **[2]**   c) **[3]**   d) **[4]**

Reading Comprehension 2

Answer the following questions in a complete sentence.

1. What do we need to be able to properly participate in civic engagement?
   (political processes / the opportunities / to participate in / we need / to be aware of)

2. What do you think is the most serious negative factor that could hamper civic engagement?

_____

  **Video Activities**

 True or False Questions

Watch the video and check the facts. Circle T if the statement is true or F if it is false.

1. The story is about elections in Ethiopia.   [T / F]
2. Ethiopia is the richest country in Africa.   [T / F]
3. Other countries do not pay much attention to events in Ethiopia.   [T / F]
4. Public safety is the key theme of the video.   [T / F]

Comprehension Questions

Watch the video again and choose the correct answer. Read the script if necessary.

1. Which of the following is true about the prime minister of Ethiopia?
   a) The international community has recognized his achievements.
   b) His political statements are broadcast everyday.
   c) He is regarded as the richest man in Ethiopia.
   d) He has studied political science at university.

2. What is one of the problems in Ethiopia highlighted by the international community?
   a) The lack of kindergartens and elementary schools
   b) Poor public transportation infrastructure
   c) Severe restrictions on television broadcasting
   d) Imprisonment of opposition political leaders

3. What can you infer from the video?
   a) Ethiopia needs more humanitarian aid.
   b) Ethiopia's military forces are financially supported by neighboring countries.
   c) Ethiopia's greatest asset is advanced medical institutions and services.
   d) Ethiopia has been successfully developing friendly diplomatic relations with neighboring countries.

Ethiopia will vote in twice-delayed elections on June 21, despite growing concern over the credibility of the vote. International attention is much more focused on an ongoing war in the country's Tigray region, where famine is affecting [1](   ) people. Prime Minister Abiy Ahmed promised the vote will be the most democratic in the history of Africa's second most populous nation.

Abiy Ahmed: "Our issue isn't protecting Ethiopia's unity. Rather it is making Ethiopia the strength of the Horn of Africa."

Thirty seven million people will be able to [2](   ) their vote on Monday, with Abiy's ruling Prosperity Party favorites to win. Abiy was awarded the 2019 Nobel Peace Prize for his efforts in ending the conflict with neighboring Eritrea. The prize came after his first year and a half in power, a time marked by optimism and promises of sweeping reforms, some successful. But as a new election [3](   ), that surge of hope has diminished. Chief among the challenges is the grueling conflict in Tigray in the north, where the vote will not take place. Fighting is still [4](   ), seven months after Ahmed sent troops to oust the region's dissident ruling party. The humanitarian situation here is dire. The UN says 91 percent of residents are in urgent need of food aid.

James Elder: "Without humanitarian access to scale up our response, an estimated 30,000-plus severely malnourished children in those highly inaccessible areas are at high risk of death."

Elsewhere in the north, Amhara state also suffers from food insecurity. And like much of the country, it has also seen an increase in ethnic violence. Ethiopia's two largest ethnic groups, the Oromo and the Amhara, frequently clash. Here too there won't be any voting. [5](   ) these conflicts are the unfortunate off-spin of the Prime Minister's break with an authoritarian past.

Agagenew Mekete: "There has been a looseness after Abiy came to office, in the name of widening the democracy."

Several international players have voiced concerns. The United States has condemned the imprisonment of opposition leaders. Most notably Eskinder Nega, a long-term government critic who was jailed in September last year on terrorism charges.

Exchanging Ideas and Thoughts

Practice the conversation with your partner. Think about how you can develop the conversation further.

A: (1) 「人は一人では生きられない」と思いますか _____
_____?

B: I do. I think that society depends on people supporting each other, and when you think about it, we are connected now more than ever before.

A: Do you mean because of social media and social networks?

B: Yes. Nowadays, (2) 知り合いと簡単にニュースを共有することができます _____
_____, and we can join social groups that reflect our interests or values.

A: That's true. And I think it is empowering to use social media positively if we say what we think and build meaningful relationships.

B: I really think that's what social media should be for. Not to just share photos of what we are doing but to really communicate with others.

Further Activity

(1) Visit the following website to learn about election-related issues. Take notes and share some interesting facts and figures you find with your classmates.

Office of the High Commissioner for Human Rights (OHCHR) , OCHCR and elections and human rights

 https://www.ohchr.org/en/elections

(2) Using key words and/or phrases you have learned from the reading and video, try Cinii Research or a similar information retrieval system to find some books and articles that are of interest to you. Compare your list of books and articles with your classmates' lists.

▼ Introduction

日々の生活を快適に送るには住宅環境が整っていることとあわせて自然環境が豊かであることも重要です。普段意識しない空気や水も汚染されるとたちまち健康被害につながります。このユニットではウェルビーイングから見た環境の大切さについて考えます。

▶▶ Warm Up Quizzes: Learning the Basics

Complete the sentences below and learn the basics about environmental quality in terms of well-being.

(1) Quality of life is _____ affected by the surrounding physical environment.

   (A) strong   (B) strongly   (C) strength   (D) strengthen

(2) Most people value the beauty and cleanliness of the place _____ they live.

   (A) that   (B) which   (C) where   (D) there

(3) People directly _____ from environmental assets and services, such as water, sanitation services, clear air, lands, forests, and access to green spaces.

   (A) benefit   (B) bestow   (C) belong   (D) behave

(4) _____ environmental and natural resources is one of the most important challenges for ensuring the sustainability of well-being over time.

   (A) Preserve   (B) Preserves   (C) Preserved   (D) Preserving

Reading Activities

Read the following passage.

1 Living in clean and comfortable housing equipped with major home appliances is not all that's necessary to ensure well-being. Environmental quality is also a key factor for quality of life. *Environmental quality* refers to the state of our
5 natural surroundings, and includes the air we breathe, the water we drink, the land we inhabit, and the overall ecological balance. The condition of the environment directly influences our physical health, our mental and emotional well-being, and our efforts to construct social harmony. **[1]** Recognizing
10 and prioritizing environmental quality is essential to enact sustainable development, and to preserve natural resources for future generations.

2 One of the most fundamental aspects of environmental quality is clean air. Breathing in polluted air can lead to respiratory
15 diseases, allergies, and other health issues. Research has consistently linked poor air quality to increased rates of asthma, lung cancer, and cardiovascular problems. **[2]** Clean air not only benefits individuals but also contributes to the collective health and productivity of communities.

20 **3** The availability of clean and safe water is equally important for human well-being. **[3]** To ensure a sustainable water supply and maintain the health of ecosystems, protecting the water quality of rivers is crucial. Contamination of water sources from industrial waste, agricultural runoff, sewage, and improper
25 waste disposal can introduce harmful substances and pathogens into the water supply. Consuming or coming into contact with polluted water can result in infection with waterborne diseases such as cholera, typhoid, dysentery, and hepatitis. Moreover, exposure to pollutants in water can lead to serious long-term
30 health problems, such as developmental disorders during childhood, organ damage, and an increased risk of certain cancers. **[4]** In addition to the direct impact on physical health, water pollution can also disrupt ecosystems, leading to a loss of aquatic biodiversity as well as ecosystem services that contribute
35 to human well-being.

4 A multi-pronged approach to maintain and improve environmental quality is necessary. First, strict regulations on

equip	備える
home appliance	家電製品
surroundings	環境
breathe	呼吸する
inhabit	住む、居住する
social harmony	社会の調和
prioritize	優先する
enact	実践する
natural resources	天然資源
polluted	汚染された
respiratory	呼吸器系の
allergy	アレルギー
link	関連づける
asthma	喘息
lung cancer	肺がん
cardiovascular	循環器の、心臓の
collective	集団の、全体の
contamination	汚染
industrial waste	産業廃棄物
agricultural runoff	農業排水
sewage	下水、汚水
improper	不適切な
waste disposal	廃棄物処理
harmful	有害な
pathogen	病原体
consume	消費する、使う
waterborne disease	水系感染症
cholera	コレラ
typhoid	腸チフス
dysentery	赤痢
hepatitis	肝炎
exposure	触れること
disrupt	破壊する
aquatic	水中の、水生の
biodiversity	生物多様性
multipronged	多方面からの

industrial emissions must be implemented, and the adoption of clean technologies must be accelerated. Second, sustainable consumption and production patterns must be practiced. Also, promoting environmental education to foster an understanding
5 of the importance of environmental protection is crucial. For our well-being and the well-being of generations to come, factors that affect environmental quality must be addressed without delay.

implement 履行する、実行する
accelerate 早める、促進する

address 取り組む

 ## Reading Comprehension 1

Read through the text and choose the correct answer.

1. What is the passage mainly about?

   a) Some attempts by private corporations to preserve the natural environment

   b) The global issues of deforestation and desertification

   c) The influence of the environment on our well-being

   d) Governmental regulations to protect water resources

2. What two environmental factors are mentioned in the passage?

   a) Air and water   b) Sunlight and wind

   c) Mountains and beaches d) Rivers and oceans

3. What is mentioned as a cause of water resource contamination?

   a) Development of residential areas

   b) Wastewater generated from farming activities

   c) Development of home appliances

   d) Construction of commercial facilities

4. In which position from [1] to [4] does the following sentence best fit?

   "Conversely, access to clean air promotes better respiratory health, reduces the risk of diseases, and enhances overall well-being."

   a) [1]   b) [2]   c) [3]   d) [4]

 ## Reading Comprehension 2

Answer the following questions in a complete sentence.

1. How does education contribute to the preservation of environmental quality?
   (to understand / the importance / it / of / people / helps / environmental protection)

2. Which factor of environmental quality is the most important for your own well-being?

_____

▶▷ True or False Questions

Watch the video and check the facts. Circle T if the statement is true or F if it is false.

1. The story is mainly about how fishing impacts water resource quality.   [T / F]
2. Due to water contamination, fishing in the river has been banned.   [T / F]
3. Small fish are affected more by water contamination.   [T / F]
4. People living along the river have faced fuel shortages.   [T / F]

▶▷ Comprehension Questions

Watch the video again and choose the correct answer. Read the script if necessary.

1. Which of the following is true about fishing on the Nile river?
   a) It has been increasing in popularity among young people.
   b) People need an official license to engage in fishing.
   c) Innovative technology will make it more lucrative.
   d) It was better in the past.

2. What do you know about the cause of water pollution?
   a) People living along the river have no idea what causes water pollution.
   b) According to a politician, there is one major source of pollution.
   c) Different kinds of waste are being dumped in the river.
   d) The government has already implemented new regulations.

3. What is NOT true about the story in the video?
   a) Due to water contamination, people must install water purifiers in their homes.
   b) Medical facilities and consumers are dumping waste into the river.
   c) The release of chemicals into the river from factories is one of the causes of water pollution.
   d) Fishing is directly affected by water pollution.

▶ Watch the video and complete the script.

Africa's longest river is under threat. Jowali has been fishing on the Nile for ¹(   ), but industrial waste dumped into the water is having a devastating effect on the river's ecosystem.

Jowali Kitegenda: "These factories are pouring the chemicals that they use in
5   animal hide processing and it is killing a lot of young fish. And the factories always release the chemicals when it is raining and a lot of fish die."

Those living along the river are ²(   ) like in Uganda, in towns like Jinja, where many are concerned for their livelihoods, as fish stocks continue to deplete year by year. Some have already ³(   ) the
10 trade.

Ali Tabo: "I imagine that time will come when people will stop coming here to fish. There will be a waste of time. They will spend like three days with nothing to catch and go home empty handed."
"The reason why we were given boreholes is because of the river water.
15   There was a time when water changed and people couldn't use it for cooking or for bathing because even after shower your skin would itch. And even fish started dying because of the toxins."

And it isn't just chemicals polluting the water. Other kinds of waste and
⁴(   ) is also finding its way into the river.

20 **Dr. Callist Tindimugaya:** "Actually pollution is probably going to be our biggest problem. We can talk about the amount of water available, but pollution is going to be a very big problem. Why? We are getting even new polluters. For example, we are getting medical waste, right now we have oil and gas. We have been having electronics. Right now we are concerned, for example,
25   when people use computers and printers, where do they dump them and what is the impact?"

A report published by the Nile basin Initiative has ⁵(   ) that untreated water, pesticides and fertilizers dumped into the river are an unprecedented threat to the area's biodiversity. And with little infrastructure in
30 place to properly clean the water, the issue will likely worsen for both humans and the environment all along the mighty Nile.

Exchanging Ideas and Thoughts

Practice the conversation with your partner. Think about how you can develop the conversation further.

A: My little brother has asthma, so (1) きれいな空気が大切なのはわかります

_____.

B: I see. Is his asthma quite serious?

A: Well, it's not bad, but he does have to carry around an asthma inhaler at all times.

B: What's an inhaler?

A: It's a small aerosol spray used when you get an asthma attack.

B: Oh, I see. It's only when we experience real health problems like that that we become more conscious of protecting the environment. Otherwise, (2) きれいな空気と水は当たり前だと思ってしまいますね _____

_____?

 Further Activity

(1) Visit the following website to learn about environmental issues worldwide. Take notes and share some interesting facts and figures that you find with your classmates.

UN Environment Programme, Publications & data

 https://www.unep.org/publications-data

(2) Using key words and/or phrases you have learned from the reading and video, try Cinii Research or a similar information retrieval system to find some books and articles that are of interest to you. Compare your list of books and articles with your classmates' lists.

12 Personal Security

治安と防犯

▼ Introduction

収入や資産が安定していて、設備の整った住居があり、社会基盤や自然環境が整っていても
ウェルビーイングが脅かされることがあります。このユニットでは人が社会生活をしていく
上で無視することのできない治安の重要性と犯罪の恐ろしさについて考えます。

▶▶ Warm Up Quizzes: Learning the Basics

Complete the sentences below and learn the basics about personal security in terms
of well-being.

(1) Living in safe _____ is essential to people's well-being.

    (A) communities (B) competitions (C) complexes   (D) compositions

(2) Feelings of insecurity have a negative _____ on how people function in daily life.

    (A) admit   (B) split   (C) impact   (D) permit

(3) Crime is one of the most common factors that _____ decisions about personal
security.

    (A) influence   (B) influences   (C) influential   (D) influencing

(4) Crime may lead to loss of life, destruction of _____, physical pain, post-traumatic
stress disorder and anxiety.

    (A) proposal   (B) prospect   (C) property   (D) projection

Reading Activities

Read the following passage.

1 Personal security is an important part of well-being because it affects our peace of mind, quality of life, and overall happiness. First and foremost, feeling secure is a key factor of personal security and well-being. Feeling safe in your own home, your own
5 neighborhood, and in other public spaces is essential to being able to lead a fulfilling life. When you feel protected from physical harm, you can focus on personal growth, building relationships, and pursuing your own aspirations. Conversely, a lack of security breeds fear, anxiety, and can hinder full participation in society.

10 **2** In contrast to feeling secure, physical security is concerned with the physical safeguarding of public spaces, infrastructure, and critical assets. A secure environment ensures that individuals can freely access essential services, such as education, healthcare, and transportation, without fear of harm
15 or disruption. **[1]** Physical security promotes social cohesion, economic development, and fosters a sense of trust and stability within communities.

3 Financial security is another vital aspect of well-being that is a component of personal security. Economic stability, job
20 security, and access to basic resources are crucial for individuals and families to thrive. **[2]** Financial insecurity can lead to stress, anxiety, and a diminished sense of well-being. Adequate social safety nets, equal economic opportunities, and responsible financial practices contribute to the sense of financial security
25 and well-being of individuals and communities.

4 In today's interconnected world, digital security has become increasingly important. The rapid advancement of technology has revolutionized how we live, work, and communicate. However, it has also introduced new vulnerabilities and risks.
30 **[3]** Cybersecurity measures, data protection laws, and digital literacy efforts are essential to ensure the security and privacy of individuals in the digital age.

5 What threatens security is crime. Crime creates an environment of fear, insecurity, and mistrust, which directly
35 affects people's quality of life and overall sense of well-being. **[4]** The consequences of high crime rates extend beyond immediate victims and can have far-reaching social, economic, and psychological effects.

---

peace of mind 安心感、心の安らぎ
foremost 一番最初に

harm 危害
focus on ～に重点を置く
aspiration 願望、抱負
conversely 逆に
lack of ～の欠如
breed 作り出す、引き起こす
fear 恐怖、恐れ
be concerned with ～に関係している
safeguard 守る、保護する
critical asset 重要な資産
disruption 混乱
cohesion 団結
trust 信頼、信用
stability 安定
vital きわめて重要な
thrive 成功する、繁栄する
diminish 減らす
adequate 十分な

interconnected 相互に関係のある
advancement 進歩
revolutionize 急進的に変える
vulnerability 脆弱性
cybersecurity サイバーセキュリティ
digital literacy デジタル技術を適切に利用できること
threaten 脅かす
mistrust 不信、疑惑
immediate 直接の
far-reaching 広範囲に及ぶ

6 One of the most evident ways in which crime affects well-being is through the harm it inflicts on individuals. Victims of crimes may experience physical injuries, emotional trauma, and psychological distress, which can have long-lasting effects
5 on their well-being. The fear of becoming a victim of crime or the experience of witnessing criminal activity can also lead to heightened anxiety, stress, and a reduced sense of personal security. This constant state of alertness and fear can erode quality of life and hinder individuals from engaging fully in their
10 daily activities. Needless to say, it is crucial to enhance public security and create safer environments for every member of a community.

inflict 与える、負わせる

witness 目撃する
heightened 増大した、高まった
alertness 警戒心、用心深さ

needless to say 言うまでもなく

▶▷ Reading Comprehension 1

Read through the text and choose the correct answer.

1. What is NOT mentioned in the passage?
    a) Having safe neighborhoods and public spaces is essential.
    b) Physical security must be considered separately from financial security.
    c) Physical security, financial security, and digital security are all important for our overall well-being.
    d) When you do not feel secure, it is difficult to work on self-development.

2. According to the text, which of the following is true about digital security?
    a) Privacy can no longer be guaranteed.
    b) It is a subset of financial security.
    c) Many countries have implemented digital-security-related laws.
    d) There are new security risks due to advances in technology.

3. The word "evident" in paragraph 6, line 1, means
    a) Difficult to understand
    b) Clearly seen
    c) Easily recorded
    d) Technologically advanced

4. In which position from [1] to [4] does the following sentence best fit?
    "Protecting our digital identities, personal information, and online transactions is vital for maintaining our well-being."
    a) [1]   b) [2]   c) [3]   d) [4]

Reading Comprehension 2

Answer the following questions in a complete sentence.

1. What kind of climate do high crime rates create in society?
   (of / creates / It / fear and mistrust / an environment).

_____

2. What aspect of security do you think is the most important to you?

_____

 Video Activities

 True or False Questions

Watch the video and check the facts. Circle T if the statement is true or F if it is false.

1. The story is from a region in Central Africa. [T / F]
2. The story is about the development of new agricultural techniques. [T / F]
3. Army forces have been deployed to protect public security. [T / F]
4. People are struggling to make a living while facing high rates of crime. [T / F]

 Comprehension Questions

Watch the video again and choose the correct answer. Read the script if necessary.

1. How do threats and thefts affect the peanut farmers?
   a) They have to purchase expensive agricultural equipment.
   b) They must ask army forces to protect the routes to the market.
   c) They have to sell their products at low prices.
   d) They have to process peanuts before selling.

2. What is one of the issues peanut farmers have to address now?
   a) There is no way to contact army forces.
   b) There is currently no public transportation to the market place.
   c) Some farmers are members of gangs.
   d) They do not have enough seeds to plant for the following year.

3. What problem is NOT mentioned in the video?
   a) The number of markets has been restricted due to threats of theft.
   b) Farmers do not have enough money to purchase new processing equipment.
   c) Supply and demand of peanuts is unbalanced.
   d) Young people do not want to be farmers.

▶ Watch the video and complete the script.

🔊 Audio 2-08

Peanuts are key for the survival of the inhabitants of Central African Republic's Paoua region. But for many growers, life is a daily ¹(   ). A good harvest should come as
5 good news. But to sell it, they must overcome theft, extortion or worse in a region where rebels and pro-government forces are at war.

Célestine Inforo: "This year, with the insecurity, there were too many threats and thefts.
10 We had to sell the production very quickly and at low prices. Now we lack seeds to replant."

Célestine Inforo is a groundnut farmer. Célestine's harvest fills ²(   ) large
15 bags of up to 45 kilogrammes in just a few hours. Then they go to a secure storeroom loaned by the humanitarian organisation Oxfam, where they are weighed and sorted. Production greatly exceeds demand in the region, which
20 drives prices down. But the growers won't dare venture as far as the capital Bangui, some ³(   ) kilometres away, to sell them. They fear attacks by rebel groups. Driven back from large towns, the rebels wage a guerilla war in the countryside.

Jean-Paul Ndopaye: "We have to transport this to either Berbérati, Bangui or
25 Bouar to sell it. But as there is this threat of highway robbers, we will be forced to sell at low prices."

A bag like this is sold for around ⁴(   ) dollars in Paoua, as little as a third of the price in Bangui. One solution is processing the peanuts and selling them at a higher price. But extracting the oil by hand is exhausting, and the locals do
30 not have the capital to invest in modern equipment.

Moussa Issoufou: "Processing is still at a really artisanal stage. We really need to try to support the chain and the industry to develop this processing and try to create outlets."

The need is great. Two thirds of the people in the region lack food,
35 ⁵(   ) the World Food Programme.

74

Exchanging Ideas and Thoughts

Practice the conversation with your partner. Think about how you can develop the conversation further.

A: I bought a new computer. (1) デジタルセキュリティーについて何かアドバイスはあります か _____?

B: Good question. I'd say it's important to keep software up-to-date, and (2) パスワード は定期的に変えるべきです _____

_____.

A: That's good advice. And do you think it's necessary to buy anti-virus software?

B: Well, it's probably worth it to protect your new computer.

A: I know, but it's so expensive.

B: It might be pricey, but it's still better than losing your data or having to buy a new computer.

Further Activity

(1) Visit the following website to learn about activities by World Food Programme. Take notes and share interesting facts and figures you find with your classmates.

World Food Programme, Where we work

 https://www.wfp.org/countries

(2) Using key words and/or phrases you have learned from the reading and video, try Cinii Research or a similar information retrieval system to find some books and articles that are of interest to you. Compare your list of books and articles with your classmates' lists.

Unit 13 Education

生涯教育

▼ Introduction

新しい知識や技術を学ぶ経験は一人ひとりの生活を豊かにするものです。またコミュニティーにとっても社会貢献ができる人材を育てることは大切です。このユニットでは、識字や生涯教育を中心に教育の重要性について考えます。

▶▶ Warm Up Quizzes: Learning the Basics

Complete the sentences below and learn the basics about education in terms of well-being.

(1) Education provides a wide _____ of benefits to society.

   (A) range   (B) rate   (C) ration   (D) random

(2) Education brings important economic _____ in the form of higher productivity and economic growth.

   (A) returning   (B) returned   (C) to be returned   (D) returns

(3) Educational attainment is strongly influenced by the _____ and socio-economic background of students' families.

   (A) infancy   (B) incident   (C) income   (D) indicator

(4) Some activities that bring intrinsic _____ to individuals, such as reading a book or writing a story, are learned as part of formal education.

   (A) pledge   (B) pleasure   (C) place   (D) plight

Reading Activities

Audio 2-09

Read the following passage.

1 The impact of education extends far beyond acquiring the knowledge and skills necessary for advancement in society. Education is the foundation for intellectual development, and it promotes personal growth. It has a profound influence on major
5　aspects of well-being such as physical and mental health. And it allows people to develop new social connections and access economic opportunities, which together can significantly enhance well-being.

2 Formal education provides people with opportunities for
10　structured intellectual development. In formal education, critical thinking skills such as reasoning and problem-solving are taught, so that individuals are equipped with the tools they need to analyze and understand the world around them. Intellectual curiosity is enhanced, and students are instilled with a life-
15　long love of learning. This intellectual development leads to a sense of self-fulfillment, personal achievement, and a greater understanding of oneself and others. **[1]**

3 Education is also a critical determinant of economic success and financial well-being. It equips people with the skills and
20　qualifications necessary to access better employment opportunities, higher incomes, and improved socioeconomic conditions. Education fosters economic mobility, reduces income inequality, and enhances our overall standard of living. **[2]** By providing us with economic stability and security, education positively affects not only our own
25　well-being but also that of our families.

4 Through education, people can acquire literacy skills (the ability to read and write), which are fundamental to being able to participate as a full member of society. Being literate empowers individuals to stay informed about current events, expand their
30　knowledge base, and make informed decisions about their lives. Furthermore, individuals are better able to navigate the world, understand their rights and responsibilities, and access essential services and opportunities. **[3]** Because literacy is essential to participate as a full member of society, it is a crucial factor of
35　well-being.

5 Formal learning contexts like school and university are not the only places that can provide valid learning opportunities. **[4]** The

---

extend　広がる、伸びる
acquire　獲得する、習得する
knowledge　知識
intellectual　知的な、知能の
profound　大きな、深い
economic　経済的な

critical thinking　批判的思考
problem-solving　問題解決 (の)
be equipped with　～を身に着けている、～を備えている
curiosity　好奇心
instill　教えこむ

fulfillment　充実 (感)
achievement　成果、功績
determinant　決定要因
equip A with B　AにBという力をつける
qualification　資格
socioeconomic　社会経済的な
inequality　不平等、不公平
standard of living　生活水準
literacy　識字
empower　力を与える
stay informed　情報に通じている
current　現在の
informed decision　情報を得たうえでの決定
navigate　しっかり進む
rights and responsibilities　権利と義務

context　環境、状況

continuous pursuit of knowledge and skills throughout one's life is called lifelong learning, and it includes self-directed learning, personal growth, and the acquisition of new competencies in non-formal learning contexts. Lifelong learning fosters cognitive
5 flexibility and critical thinking skills, and encourages us to explore new subjects, ideas, and perspectives for ourselves. It is important for both society and individuals to recognize the importance of providing learning opportunities to gain new knowledge and skills, and the value of continuing education through life.

continuous	継続的な
lifelong learning	生涯学習
competence	能力
flexibility	柔軟性
explore	探求する、調べる
subject	主題、テーマ
perspective	考え方、視点
gain	得る、獲得する

 Reading Comprehension 1

Read through the text and choose the correct answer.

1. Which of the following points is mentioned in the passage?
   a) Acquiring knowledge is more important than improving physical skills.
   b) Educational performance depends on physical health.
   c) Educational achievement has little to do with one's wealth or income.
   d) Education is important for financial success.

2. What is true about literacy?
   a) It is a fundamental public service.   b) It is a form of critical thinking.
   c) It enables people to understand   d) It provides economic stability.
      written language.

3. The phrase "lifelong learning" in paragraph 5, line 4, means
   a) The continuous pursuit of knowledge and skills throughout one's life
   b) Education courses designed for adults and senior citizens
   c) Complimentary educational services provided by local government
   d) Accessibility to information provided by sources such as the Internet

4. In which position from **[1]** to **[4]** does the following sentence best fit?
   "For example, literacy enables individuals to access and comprehend information from diverse sources such as books, newspapers, online platforms, and other educational resources."
   a) **[1]**   b) **[2]**   c) **[3]**   d) **[4]**

 Reading Comprehension 2

Answer the following questions in a complete sentence.

1. Why are 'social connections' and 'economic opportunities' mentioned in the first paragraph? (They are mentioned / the impact / on well-being / as examples of / that / education has).

2. With regard to financial well-being, what do you think is the most important educational outcome?

_____

  **Video Activities**

▶▷ True or False Questions

Watch the video and check the facts. Circle T if the statement is true or F if it is false.

1. The video is about a school in the countryside.   [**T** / **F**]
2. The video is about the relationship between people's age and how   [**T** / **F**]
   much they sleep.
3. There are not enough teachers at elementary schools in the region.   [**T** / **F**]
4. The youngest learner in the video is 29 years old.   [**T** / **F**]

▶▷ Comprehension Questions

Watch the video again and choose the correct answer. Read the script if necessary.

1. What do the learners in the video want to do?
   a) They want to financially support their family members.
   b) They want to acquire the ability to read and write.
   c) They want to build a school for their children.
   d) They want to work as volunteer teachers.

2. What can you infer from the video?
   a) Girls lacked opportunities to attend school.
   b) Children in India tend to perform well academically.
   c) The compulsory education system in India has a good reputation in South Asia.
   d) The literacy rate in rural parts of India is high.

3. What do you know about the school uniform?
   a) It is provided for free by local government.
   b) Learners do not have to wear school uniforms.
   c) The color of the uniform represents equality within the community.
   d) It is made by a local volunteer organization.

Learning to read and write at a unique school in ¹(   ) India. These
women are all aged between 60 and ²(   )
and are finally fulfilling their life-long
dream of becoming literate.

5 **Gulab Kedar:** "I never went to school as a
child. It feels great to come now and
study with my friends."

As children, these women stayed at home or worked ³(   )
their brothers got an education. Now, for two hours every day, they come to
10 "Grandmothers' School," as it is known in
the local Marathi language.

Kantanbai More: "When we used to go to
the bank, we had to give thumb prints.
It was embarrassing and there was a
15 stigma attached. Now I feel proud and
happy because I can sign my name."

The school, ⁴(   ) kilometres from
Mumbai, is funded by a charitable trust and
marks its first anniversary this year. The
20 man behind the initiative says the school,
including its colorful uniform, is challenging
traditional attitudes and can be an example
to other villages.

Yogendra Bangar: "Most of the grandmothers are widows and are meant to
25 wear white while mourning. We wanted to break this taboo and other
older traditions to make every person feel they are equal and part of the
community, without any discrimination on the basis of poor or rich, so pink
was chosen."

Come the end of the day, it's time to head off for the 29 pupils. Often
30 there's homework to be done, sometimes with a little help from the
⁵(   ).

Exchanging Ideas and Thoughts

Practice the conversation with your partner. Think about how you can develop the conversation further.

A: Can I ask a question— (1) なぜ大学に入学したのですか _____

_____?

B: (2) 卒業後に良い仕事につけるように入学しました _____

_____. And you?

A: Same as you. But I'm also really enjoying study. Actually, I'm in a study group right now, and we review notes from lectures together. It's helping me a lot.

B: You set up your own study group? You must be very motivated to study.

A: Well, I find that studying with friends motivates me to study more. You should come along to our next study session tomorrow!

B: Yes, I'd like to. It actually sounds kind of fun.

Further Activity

(1) Visit the following website to learn about education-related issues worldwide. Take notes and share some interesting facts and figures you find with your classmates.

 UNESCO, UNESCO's action in education

 https://www.unesco.org/en/education/action

(2) Using key words and/or phrases you have learned from the reading and video, try Cinii Research or a similar information retrieval system to find some books and articles that are of interest to you. Compare your list of books and articles with your classmates' lists.

Social Connection

人との繋がり

▼ Introduction

豊かな人生を送るには人との繋がりが欠かせません。このユニットでは、コミュニティーとのつながり、人と人とのつながりの重要性を踏まえた上で、交流の場の実践例について知識を深め考えます。

▶▶ Warm Up Quizzes: Learning the Basics

Complete the sentences below and learn the basics about making social connections and how they are related to well-being.

(1) Frequency of contact with others and quality of personal relationships _____ crucial determinants of people's well-being.

    (A) is   (B) has   (C) are   (D) have

(2) People derive intrinsic pleasure from spending time with _____.

    (A) other   (B) another   (C) the other   (D) others

(3) People _____ extensive social support networks have better health outcomes and tend to live longer.

    (A) about   (B) on   (C) with   (D) among

(4) Well-developed social connections can _____ trust in other people, tolerance of diversity and norms of reciprocity.

    (A) generate   (B) collaborate   (C) incorporate   (D) deteriorate

Read the following passage.

1 Human beings are social animals. We intrinsically seek connection with others throughout our lifespan. Whether it's with family, friends, romantic partners, or larger communities, making social connections provides numerous benefits that
5 significantly influence our overall well-being.

2 One of the primary benefits of making social connections is the positive effect it has on our mental and emotional health. When we have meaningful relationships and interactions with others, we experience a sense of belonging, acceptance, and support.
10 While loneliness and isolation tend to have a negative impact on our mental and emotional state, positive social interaction is beneficial because it reduces stress and increases happiness.

3 In addition, research has shown that individuals with strong social connections have lower rates of anxiety, depression, and
15 other mental health disorders. Having someone to confide in and share your thoughts and feelings with not only provides emotional comfort but can also help you to find solutions to problems you may be experiencing. In times of crisis or adversity, social support becomes even more important, because it acts as a
20 buffer against the negative effects of stress and helps individuals cope better in challenging situations.

4 Furthermore, having a social support network contributes to physical well-being. Research has indicated that individuals with strong social ties tend to lead healthier lifestyles. People are more
25 likely to engage in regular exercise, maintain a balanced diet, and adhere to medical advice. These behaviors can have a significant impact on reducing the risk of chronic diseases, improving cardiovascular health, and enhancing overall physical fitness.

5 In today's society, however, developing social connections can
30 be challenging due to factors such as busy schedules, digital distractions, and the prevalence of virtual interactions. To cultivate meaningful relationships, you should keep the following pointers in mind: **[1]** First, prioritize face-to-face interactions. Scheduling regular face-to-face meetings, dinners, or coffee dates with family,
35 friends, and acquaintances will strengthen your relationships. **[2]** Second, engage in social activities or join interest-based groups to develop social connections. **[3]** Third, attend community events

social animal	社会的な動物
intrinsically	もともと、本質的に
lifespan	人生、一生
primary	主な、主要な
meaningful	意味のある
interaction	交流、意思の疎通
a sense of belonging	帰属意識、一体感
health disorder	健康障害
confide in	打ち明ける
comfort	快適さ、安らぎ
crisis	危機、重大局面
adversity	逆境、苦難
social support	社会的支援、ソーシャルサポート
act as	～として機能する
buffer	緩和剤
cope	対処する、取り組む
challenging	大変な、困難な
social ties	社会的なつながり
engage in	参加する、携わる
adhere to	守る
cardiovascular	心血管系の
physical fitness	体の健康、体力
distraction	娯楽
prevalence	普及、流行
cultivate	育む、育てる
pointer	指針
face-to-face	対面の、直接の
acquaintance	知人、知り合い
strengthen	強くする
interest-based group	趣味の集まり

such as festivals, markets, workshops, and cultural gatherings because they provide a useful platform to meet new people. Go to as many as you can. [4] Fourth, be patient and persistent because developing social connections requires both time and effort. If you
5 follow these recommendations, the relationships you develop will enhance your mental and physical health and provide unique opportunities for you to learn and grow. Prioritizing well-being means developing the social connections that will help you to stay healthy and productive in today's busy world.

gathering	集会、集まり
platform	土台、舞台
patient	忍耐強い、辛抱強い
persistent	根気強い

Reading Comprehension 1

Read through the text and choose the correct answer.

1. What does the second paragraph describe?

   a) The relationship between developing strong social connections and health

   b) The relationship between developing strong social connections and income

   c) How to interact with others in a more meaningful way

   d) The definition of social connections

2. What is NOT mentioned as an example of a healthy lifestyle?

   a) Taking medical advice   b) Exercising regularly

   c) Getting mental health counseling   d) Having a balanced diet

3. What could hamper the development of healthy social connections?

   a) Investing in the stock market   b) Having routine medical checkups

   c) Paying high consumption tax   d) Getting immersed in online gaming

4. In which position from **[1]** to **[4]** does the following sentence best fit?

   "For example, joining a sports team, a book club, a volunteering organization, or a hobby group will provide you with chances to interact with others."

   a) **[1]**   b) **[2]**   c) **[3]**   d) **[4]**

Reading Comprehension 2

Answer the following questions in a complete sentence.

1. What is an advantage of developing healthy social connections?
   (can help / solutions to problems / challenging situations / us / social connections / find / in)

2. Which kind of face-to-face interaction do you prefer?

  Video Activities

▶▷ True or False Questions

Watch the video and check the facts. Circle T if the statement is true or F if it is false.

1. The setting of the video is a café.   [T / F]
2. The café in the video provides language lectures.   [T / F]
3. Old people tend to get emotional when they tell a story.   [T / F]
4. People gather in a café to share their experiences.   [T / F]

▶▷ Comprehension Questions

Watch the video again and choose the correct answer. Read the script if necessary.

1. What do you know about the café in the video?

   a) It is a place for visitors to share their stories about a specific experience.

   b) People have to be registered members to enter the café.

   c) It does not provide dinner.

   d) It offers free tea and coffee to visitors.

2. What did you learn about the interaction at the café?

   a) Visitors can enjoy a story hour by a professional storyteller.

   b) Some people come to the café to read books, magazines, and newspapers.

   c) Recreational activities, such as board games and card games, promote communication.

   d) There is a lot of laughter.

3. What does the speaker recommend people to do?

   a) People should arrange times to have face-to-face conversations.

   b) People should not be afraid to talk about death.

   c) People should spend more time interacting than having soft drinks and snacks.

   d) People should pay more attention to the comfort of their surroundings.

▶ Watch the video and complete the script.

Mireille Hayden: "Because death is a taboo, we don't talk about it, we don't plan for it. So when it happens, we're so bewildered. We don't have the language to talk about it. It's a complete shock."

5   I have been doing Death Cafés for ¹(   ) years, I have done many, I've spoken to hundreds of people and I've never had the same conversation.

Male participant: "How many words can you take to say 'has died'? 'Is dead,'
10 two words, phrases in English."

Mireille: "Some of the stories are really sad and stories of ²(   ) and stories of loss."

The experience of death is very
15 isolating and it's a time when people actually need more support. But because it's such a taboo, people don't have the language and don't know what to do. So they ³(   ) not having the conversation, not approaching somebody.

20 People come to a death cafe because they want to share that, because they want to hear other people's experiences, because they want to maybe tell a story, a difficult story around ⁴(   ).

Female participant: "It was so unbelievably devastating and difficult to be there."

Death is part of life. It's a natural part of what happens to us all and yet
25 nobody gets to talk about it because everybody says like 'oh it's too ⁵(   ), oh we shouldn't talk about it, oh it's too sad.' And actually, what we have in our death cafes is that we have a lot of laughter and that always surprises people.

What we do is we go through life as if we're never gonna die and so we're all on this treadmill, all in this rat race, and actually, with the consciousness of
30 our death, that happens when we start thinking about it, when we start talking about it, then we make the most of our finite lives.

So it's always really interesting, and it's always really quite deep and it's always also quite funny and sad.

Exchanging Ideas and Thoughts

Practice the conversation with your partner. Think about how you can develop the conversation further.

A: I think developing good social connections is the most important factor for well-being.

B: So you're saying that having meaningful relationships is more important than money and housing?

A: Yes, that's right. Money is important, but (1) 人と交流することは値段がつけられないほど貴重です _____.

B: Well, that's interesting. Personally, (2) 交流することにはあまりのめりこめません

_____. I prefer spending time with my gadgets.

A: Do you mean using your smartphone to communicate with friends?

B: No, I mean using them to play online-games, watch videos, and listen to music by myself.

 **Further Activity**

(1) Visit the following website to learn about the importance of making social connections. Try the featured source, related links and related topics to find out more about the topic. Take notes and share some interesting facts and figures you find with your classmates.

World Health Organization, Social Isolation and Loneliness

 https://www.who.int/teams/social-determinants-of-health/demographic-change-and-healthy-ageing/social-isolation-and-loneliness

(2) Using key words and/or phrases you have learned from the reading and video, try Cinii Research or a similar information retrieval system to find some books and articles that are of interest to you. Compare your list of books and articles with your classmates' lists.

Review Quiz

復習テスト

▶▷ Vocabulary Check

Match each word with its meaning.

Nouns 1

1 advancement ( )	5 impact ( )	9 fatigue ( )
2 achievement ( )	6 fuel ( )	10 debt ( )
3 bond ( )	7 vitality ( )	
4 competence ( )	8 consumption ( )	

a 能力	b 活力、活気	c 味、風味	d 成果、功績	e 影響	f 疲労、倦怠感
g 進歩	h 消費	i 燃料	j 借金、負債	k 例外	l 絆、縁

Nouns 2

11 alienation ( )	15 volatility ( )	19 aspiration ( )
12 affection ( )	16 depression ( )	20 contamination ( )
13 asthma ( )	17 deterioration ( )	
14 competence ( )	18 apathy ( )	

a 喘息	b 能力	c 無関心	d 願望、抱負	e 鬱	f 疎外感
g 満足感	h 悪化	i 愛情	j 変動性	k 栄養素	l 汚染

Verbs 1

21 address ( )	25 investigate ( )	29 extend ( )
22 diminish ( )	26 promote ( )	30 diversify ( )
23 breathe ( )	27 pursue ( )	
24 identify ( )	28 explore ( )	

a 早める、促進する	b 評価する、決める	c 特定する、認識する	d 探求する、調べる	e 広がる、伸びる	f 求める、追及する
g 減らす	h 参加する	i 分散する	j 調査する	k 取り組む	l 呼吸する

Verbs 2

31 accommodate ( )　35 intertwine ( )　39 displace ( )
32 alleviate ( )　36 empower ( )　40 cultivate ( )
33 enact ( )　37 penalize ( )
34 compromise ( )　38 prioritize ( )

a	軽減する、和らげる	b	罰する、懲らしめる	c	優先する	d	育む、育てる	e	力を与える	f	教えこむ
g	妥協する	h	実践する	i	妨害する	j	立ち退かせる	k	絡み合う	l	受け入れる

Adjectives

41 absolute ( )　45 constant ( )　49 numerous ( )
42 adequate ( )　46 vital ( )　50 patient ( )
43 cautious ( )　47 alternative ( )
44 chronic ( )　48 prompt ( )

a	十分な	b	代替の	c	数多くの	d	絶対の	e	絶えず続く	f	用心深い
g	極めて重要な	h	慢性の、習慣的な	i	予期しない	j	迅速な、素早い	k	不快な	l	辛抱強い、忍耐強い

▷▷ Basics about Well-being

(51) Well-being is the state of being physically, mentally, and emotionally healthy, content, and _____.

(A) fulfill　　　(B) fulfilled　　　(C) fulfilling　　　(D) to fulfill

(52) Money is essential for meeting basic needs such as food, shelter, healthcare, and education, and _____ a foundation for overall well-being.

(A) provide　　　(B) provides　　　(C) providing　　　(D) provided

(53) Preserving people's wealth ensures that their living standards can be _____ over time.

(A) suspected　　　(B) summoned　　　(C) supposed　　　(D) sustained

(54) A financial crisis in one country can quickly _____ to others.

    (A) spot   (B) spoil   (C) split   (D) spread

(55) Well-balanced and nutritious meals are essential for _____ health and well-being.

    (A) maintain   (B) maintained   (C) maintaining   (D) maintenance

(56) Health status directly impacts physical and mental abilities _____ quality of life.

    (A) at least   (B) more or less   (C) nonetheless   (D) as well as

(57) Mental health _____ emotional stability, cognitive functioning, relationships, self-esteem, and your overall quality of life.

    (A) influence   (B) to be influenced   (C) influencing   (D) influences

(58) Housing conditions can impact the _____, safety, and overall well-being of individuals or families.

    (A) competitor   (B) complex   (C) comfort   (D) composition

(59) Homelessness often results _____ a combination of economic, social, and personal factors.

    (A) from   (B) between   (C) among   (D) toward

(60) Civic engagement refers to the various activities that people perform to express their political _____ and contribute to the political functioning of society.

    (A) vessel   (B) value   (C) voice   (D) vitality

(61) Quality of life is _____ affected by the surrounding physical environment.

    (A) strong   (B) strongly   (C) strength   (D) strengthen

(62) Living in safe _____ is essential for people's well-being.

    (A) communities   (B) competitions   (C) complexes   (D) compositions

(63) Education provides a wide _____ of benefits to society.

    (A) range   (B) rate   (C) ration   (D) random

(64) People derive intrinsic pleasure from spending time with _____.

    (A) other   (B) another   (C) the other   (D) others

(65) Well-being is typically _____ by factors such as health, happiness, and quality of life, and these factors can be evaluated according to specific indices.

(A) determine   (B) determines   (C) determined   (D) determining

(66) Individual wealth and income are heavily dependent _____ national and regional economic conditions.

(A) from   (B) for   (C) to   (D) on

(67) The central _____ of health status in terms of well-being is physical health.

(A) component   (B) combination   (C) common   (D) commerce

(68) Housing is not just a mere shelter but is deeply intertwined _____ people's physical, mental, and social well-being.

(A) between   (B) with   (C) among   (D) into

(69) 'No man is an island' is a well-known _____, and it means that we cannot live life detached from other people.

(A) says   (B) said   (C) saying   (D) say

(70) Education _____ people to develop new social connections and access economic opportunities, which together can significantly enhance well-being.

(A) alternates   (B) alters   (C) alarms   (D) allows

Well-being: Essential Elements for Our Life
映像メディアで考えるウェルビーイング

2024 年 4 月 10 日　初版第 1 刷発行

編　著　者　　山本五郎／Craig Langford

発　行　者　　森　信久
発　行　所　　株式会社　松柏社
　　　　　　　〒102−0072　東京都千代田区飯田橋1 −6 −1
　　　　　　　TEL　03 (3230) 4813（代表）
　　　　　　　FAX　03 (3230) 4857
　　　　　　　http://www.shohakusha.com
　　　　　　　e-mail: info@shohakusha.com

装　　　帳　　小島トシノブ（NONdesign）
印刷・製本　　中央精版印刷株式会社
ISBN978-4-88198-788-9
略　　　号 = 788
Copyright © 2024 by Goro Yamamoto & Craig Langford